Dark Psychology Secrets:

Defenses Against Covert Manipulation, Mind Control, NLP, Emotional Influence, Deception, and Brainwashing

Table of Contents

Introduction 1

Chapter 1: The Art of Manipulation 7
    Goals and Intents of Manipulation 8
    Where Is Manipulation Used? 11
    Who Uses Manipulation and Dark Psychology? 11
    Why Is Learning About Manipulation Important? 13

Chapter 2: The Importance of Reading People 16
    Reading People From a Dark Psychology User's Point of View 16
    Reading People From a Potential Victim's Point of View 20

Chapter 3: Manipulation Techniques 24
    Three Modes of Persuasion 24
    Emotional Manipulation 27
    Power Play and Dominance 30
    Charm and Flattery/Mirroring 32

Chapter 4: Emotional Manipulation 36
    Short-Term Manipulation 36
    Long-Term Manipulation 38

Chapter 5: The Importance of Self-Esteem 43
    The "Ideal Woman" 43
    Build Self-Esteem Through Meditation 46
    Take Care of Your Health and Body 48
    Build a Support System 48

Chapter 6: Workplace Manipulation 52
    Using Manipulation to Climb the Corporate Ladder 52
    Using Manipulation to Defend One's Position 53
    Using Manipulation to Gain Power Over Colleagues 57

Chapter 7: Manipulative Partners 61
    Flattery and Superficial Charm 62
    Gradual Emotional Breakdown 64
    Attachment and the Fear of Loss 66

Chapter 8: Acceptable Influence vs. Toxic Manipulation 70
Tolerable Manipulation and Influence 71
Not All Intentions Are Malicious 75

Chapter 9: Manipulative Family Members 77
The Child as the Manipulator 77
The Parent as the Manipulator 81

Chapter 10: Defenses Against Brainwashing 86
How Is Brainwashing Accomplished? 86
How to Avoid Brainwashing? 92

Chapter 11: Neuro-Linguistic Programming 95
What Is NLP? 95
How is NLP Used in a Manipulation Scheme? 100

Chapter 12: Covert Mind Control 104
The Subliminal Message Experiment 104
Art of Embedded Commands 106
How to Protect Yourself From Covert Mind Control 111

Chapter 13: Recognizing Manipulators 113
They Constantly Challenge You to Prove Yourself and Show Affection 113
They Are Passive-Aggressive 114
They Use Gaslighting on You 114
They Use Humor as a Weapon Against You 115
They Are Always the Victim 115
They Use Kindness as a Weapon 115
They Belittle Your Pain 116
They Keep Their Cool to Magnify Your Own Emotions 116

Chapter 14: Manipulating Manipulators 117
Mirror the Manipulator 117
Be Immune to the Manipulator's Charms 118
Be Aware of Your Emotions 119

Conclusion 121

Introduction

Congratulations on purchasing *Dark Psychology Secrets*, and thank you for doing so.

The following chapters will discuss a great deal of information regarding the presence and usage of what is called "dark psychology," which refers to manipulative practices working under the radar of the victim in order to get the  practitioner something he or she wants. These goals might include any number of things, most of which are solely concerned with the benefit of the manipulator. And that is the danger of dark psychology—a practitioner who develops these skills and uses them on other people has zero concern with the ethics of the situation; they simply want something and are going to take a shortcut to get there. The cost of such endeavors involves emotional and psychic pain of a great many levels, and the damage from such experiences can last a lifetime, only somewhat assuaged by numerous types of therapy and treatment.

You may be surprised at the scope of techniques and tools which fall under the category and usage of dark psychology, and the scope of this book is to cover all of the major practices which you are likely to encounter at least once in your life. Many people have been used and abused by these practices without ever having realized it.

In chapter 1, we will discover the art of manipulation and how this works on the human mind in practice. We will discuss some of the foundational human tendencies which are exploited in common manipulation techniques and look at a few examples of these strategies in action.

Next, we will discuss how you can practice the skill of reading other people and the environment around you. In today's modern world, it has become easier and easier for people to work their dark psychology strategies while people are constantly distracted by their work, their phones, and their social lives through constant social media engagement, etc. How can you keep yourself alert and aware of when something might be amiss? We will give you some practical tips and tools for arming yourself against dark psychology schemes. As we will mention many times in this book, one of the best ways to arm yourself and prepare for any type of dark psychology encounters is to educate yourself on the different strategies involved, and this is the topic we will cover in chapter 3.

In chapter 4, we will discuss one of the most painful effects of dark psychology, which have to do with emotional manipulation. Learn how dark psychology practitioners exploit human emotion and the psychology of human behavior to get what they want at the expense of your emotional well-being. Learn to identify when this might be happening to you before we move on to a very important chapter on self-esteem.

One of the first steps a dark psychology practitioner takes is choosing a victim. This is done after a period of observation and evaluation, where they decide who is most likely to go along with their schemes. Targets who are vulnerable include those with low self-esteem and a high degree of naivete. You can guard yourself against being chosen by improving your self-esteem or, at the very least, conveying publicly that you are confident. Simple tools of body language and nonverbal communication can convey this message, even if you are still working on self-esteem and confidence. Behaviors as simple as holding your head up high with your shoulders back can influence whether a dark psychology user will move in on you or move on to someone else who seems easier to manipulate.

In chapter 6, we will discuss the practice of dark psychology in the workplace environment. Manipulation in this context happens all the time and, often, without the victims even knowing it. Learn to recognize when this is happening around you and trust your instincts when you get a bad feeling about an interaction.

Manipulative partners are our next subject and one which can be the most seriously damaging psychologically. This is because we are dealing with manipulation coming from a partner we love and trust.

In the next chapter, we will differentiate between what is an acceptable influence and what is toxic manipulation. As an easy example, think of the psychology used by a salesperson inside his store. When you walk into the store, you might expect some degree of interaction and a sales pitch or two directed your way. The salesman might use techniques like advertising a limited-time sale or ask you questions about your life in order to use that information in his sales pitch. This is a degree of dark psychology, though it is being used in a way that is not designed to be harmful or maliciously trick another person into the desired outcome. The customer has an ultimate say and makes the decision whether or not to buy. The customer might also dismiss the sales pitch altogether before the salesman has even started, and this is her right to do so. Things like using carefully constructed arguments to persuade others to his point of view is an acceptable form of influence while utilizing lies and inciting anger and violence in order to recruit political influence and support is an example of a toxic level of manipulation.

In chapter 9, we will discuss manipulative family members and what to do when the person manipulating you is someone you live with or have close ties to. Sometimes, it's not an option just to walk away from the situation, and you will need to have tools and strategies that you can employ in this difficult type of dark psychology situation.

Brainwashing is the topic of our next chapter. You will learn the basics and how to recognize if you or someone you know is under the influence of someone trying to employ these tactics to whatever end serves them. Though you might think you are too smart to fall under this kind of influence, many others have come forward publicly to describe how they thought the exact same way and were manipulated into belief systems and behaviors, which they never thought they could be subjected to. We are all human beings, and it is the commonalities of thought and emotion and behavior that the dark psychology user exploits.

Neuro-linguistic programming might be a term you've never heard before, but it is an important topic under the umbrella of dark psychology. Learn how behavior and thought processing can be influenced by language techniques and routine behaviors to rewire the brain.

In chapter 12, we will cover the arena of covert mind control in the form of such insidious techniques as gaslighting. In the next chapter, you will learn how to identify specific individuals in your environment who are trying to utilize dark psychology on you or others around you.

Finally, in chapter 14, we will discuss how you yourself can employ tactics of dark psychology in order to turn malicious manipulators away and to sabotage active dark psychology tactics. Learn to give such individuals a taste of their own medicine and spread this knowledge to anyone else whom you think may benefit from knowing how to stop a dark psychology user in his tracks.

There are plenty of books on this subject on the market; thanks again for choosing this one! Every effort was made to ensure it is full of as much useful information as possible. Please enjoy!

Chapter 1: The Art of Manipulation

The dictionary's definition of the word "manipulate" is "to change by artful or unfair means so as to serve one's purpose." This definition encompasses a large number of human behaviors and strategies for getting what we want, especially from other people, and the topic we will be discussing has to do with manipulation when it is done with intentional trickery that is designed to be undetected by the victim. This is what we call dark psychology.

Dark psychology is all about the human mind and changing the conditions of thought and emotion in order to get people to do things and think things they would not necessarily have of their own volition. Manipulation can be accomplished in many different ways, and it is not always accomplished consciously on the part of the user. In other words, people can behave in ways that are conducive to getting what they want from others through manipulation without having any forethought or planning to use manipulative strategies. Think of the young child who throws a tantrum or cries in an exaggerated way that is not completely genuine to get what he wants. A young child is not knowledgable in the ways of the human mind and manipulation; she just knows through experience that her mother is likely to behave in a certain way when she cries. Manipulation is tricky in this regard, as it is used and practiced everywhere and by everyone, though the intent is not always malicious and the tactics themselves are not always readily identified. For sure, people can be manipulated by an individual who then disappears after getting what they aimed to get, never to be seen again and without the victim knowing what had happened. Often, a victim only realizes much later or after experiencing manipulation when it is too late or when the bulk of the damage has already been done. So what are some of the things that motivate people to manipulate others?

Goals and Intents of Manipulation

There are certainly too many possible answers to this question to cover all of them here, but there are some general assumptions we can make in order to pinpoint the answer to why a person chooses to use manipulation and other dark psychology techniques.

We can reasonably assume that the practitioner chooses manipulation because there doesn't seem to be another way or that it is the easiest way. Manipulation might be the last resort when other, more straightforward tactics fail. But it might also be the tactics of choice for the practitioner simply because he lacks the means or capacity to accomplish his goal by more ethically sound routes. This is the case when we talk about deviant personalities, such as the narcissist. The narcissist does not have the capacity to commiserate or empathize or even feel compassion for other human beings. Therefore, he must put on the mask of someone who shares these traits in order to form relationships that will help him accomplish his goals. In this and other similar cases, manipulation is adopted as the preferred mode for interaction simply because the user does not or cannot interact in a more acceptable way. He knows that when his differences are detected, it works to push people away; therefore, dark psychology becomes a necessity and, ultimately, a way of life.

In other instances, a person of "normal" capacity for human relationships might turn to manipulation because it is an easier way to get what he wants. The user might recognize and even be able to feel the guilt or shame that might accompany the use of such tactics but chooses himself and his goals above the concern of others and/or his victims' well-being, emotional and otherwise. For example, a young man talking to a woman he is attracted to understands that when he lies to her in order to make her more amenable to a second date or get her to come home with him, he is doing so under false pretenses and that this may lead to emotional and psychological damage to the victim, but he decides that being able to sleep with her is more important to him than any concern about her feelings. Unfortunately, this occurs all the time and can result in either emotional or physical damage in the form of date rape or more long-term abuse and manipulation.

The goals of people who practice manipulation can be simple, complex, or nearly unfathomable to those who would never knowingly cause harm through the use of dark psychology. A practitioner may simply be looking for easy sexual encounters, or he might try to establish a long-term relationship in order to siphon emotional energy and practice control and dominance. The goal might be financially focused, or a position of power and influence, or the practitioner simply wants to earn admiration and rapport with others who are powerful and influential. The goals may be short-term, such as coming up with a distraction to a person walking by to pick something from his pocket. It can also be long-term,  such as the adoption of a complete alternate personality in order to lead a double life alongside another. The amount of planning and forethought varies quite a bit as well, depending on many different factors and intentions. Sometimes, it is impossible to understand fully why a dark psychology user operates the way he does. We will go as far as we can to understand the psychology underneath this mode of operation, but the main focus of this book is to teach you how to recognize the techniques and strategies at work and avoid becoming a victim yourself. These tools may save your life in the most extreme cases and if you choose to share what you have learned, the life of someone close to you.

Where Is Manipulation Used?

The unfortunate truth here is that manipulation is used nearly anywhere, as long as there are people to manipulate; it's as simple as that. No person nor the environment is necessarily safe from such practice because manipulation itself is something both innate in all human beings to some degree and easily developed as a life skill for those who choose to use manipulation as part of their survival on a regular basis. Sometimes, it is used for the purpose of pleasure. We all use manipulation to some degree at some point over the course of our lives, and this occurs in any environment where we interact with other people. The difference between you and those who practice malicious dark psychology tactics is that their intents are focused and amped to the highest intensity possible to ensure that they are exercising as much influence as possible to fundamentally change the victim's mind for a period of time. The question is about the degree to which dark psychology tactics are used, and this book is all about protecting you from its most insidious and malicious forms.

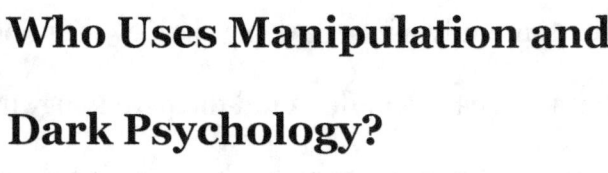

Who Uses Manipulation and Dark Psychology?

Those who use dark psychology on a deep level and on a regular basis are those who are also successful in presenting to other people a persona and demeanor completely different than the one on the inside. We've all heard a story or two about a criminal who was apprehended in a community where the individual had convinced a lot of people that he was just a kind man or a regular Joe in town. These types are often the most successful, most ruthless, and who has the longest career in terms of their criminal or psychological intents against victims.

But dark psychology is not limited, as we've discussed, to the criminally oriented or those with deviant personalities. While manipulation and dark psychology can be a way of life for some, others use it for the sake of a very specific goal. For instance, take the tragic example of a young addict who uses a cycle of manipulation on his parents in order to get something he needs to feed his habit. Perhaps he disappears for weeks at a time and only comes home when he needs money to buy more drugs. He might prey on his parents' love and need to support him by playing the part of a needy son who just needs love and support to get better. Just when the parents are convinced he is on the right path, he takes what money he can from them and leaves to repeat the cycle again until he needs more support or a place to stay. This type of cycle can occur in a number of ways and manifestations. There's the jealous lover who uses control tactics to string along a partner while engaging in an affair or pursuing other interests. There's the guy addicted to gambling, who keeps asking friends and family for money while promising them he would change just to go feed his addiction and return again. Someone addicted to empathy and attention from others might make up ailments or predicaments in order to feed that emotional need and recover only to think of another ruse when she feels needy again.

Why Is Learning About Manipulation Important?

The practice and context of dark psychology and manipulation range from the simple motivation to the very complex long-term plan. Some readers, at this very moment, suspect they may be bending to some form of dark psychology in their lives and hope to educate themselves on how to break these cycles, while others want to safeguard themselves against the possibility of dark psychology being used on them after witnessing the harmful effects of such acts on a loved one.

Contrary to many peoples' opinions, protecting yourself against dark psychology and manipulation is not just a matter of being smart and more intelligent than the next guy. Victims of manipulation are not just "too dumb" to figure out what's happening to them. Anyone who experiences emotions and thinks like a human being is a potential victim, and those who have experienced such trauma from a psychologically abusive spouse or partner or an online scam should not feel like they are just hopelessly less observant than other people. There are things you can do to improve the chances that you will recognize and be able to act before these tactics are successfully used against you in the future. One of the most important steps is something you are already doing—educating yourself on how these people work and what the tactics look like in the moments when it counts.

Remember, guarding yourself against complete strangers who might be using dark psychology on you is one thing, but it's important to remember that those you love and trust have the most power when it comes to inflicting psychological harm. The stranger who wants to use you to some end has the initial goal of creating a relationship or interaction with you where they gain your trust, but someone who is already in your life as a person you love has probably already accomplished this goal. People who are initially trustworthy, respectful, and compassionate individuals do not often switch gears and become malicious, but you must recognize that there might be key differences between the core of those whom you choose to have in your life and those who are members of your family or already part of your life in some way. The daughter whose mother is being manipulated by her stepfather may have limited influence in terms of convincing her mother that she is being used and abused, but it is worth trying to get the mother to realize, through evidence, that something is wrong with the relationship. Sometimes, however, it is up to the victims themselves to make the real change and remove themselves completely from a situation like this. You cannot always force someone into tearing away from someone they have formed a strong attachment, and one of the key tactics of manipulative partners is to sever ties between the victim and his/her family and loved ones. The idea is to make the victim's whole world revolve around the dark psychology user. With this in mind, if you suspect that someone you love is under the influence of dark psychology or manipulation with malicious intent, do not let this person tear the victim away from you if possible. Remain in their lives, no matter how much the abuser has turned the victim against you. If you recognize that the behavior is way out of character, then you can decide that there is some outside influence being injected, and this is most often accomplished through lies and complex forms of emotional and dependency manipulation. The best thing you can do is remain as close as possible to the victim until he/she is ready to realize what's happening.

If you believe someone you know is in physical danger from an abuser, it is important that you notify authorities and have law enforcement or protection agencies intervene as soon as possible.

Chapter 2: The Importance of Reading People

In this chapter, we will discuss the importance of reading people from two perspectives—the point of view of the perpetrator and that of the victim.

Reading People From a Dark Psychology User's Point of View

As mentioned previously, one of the first and most important steps a practitioner of dark psychology takes is the period of observation where he is getting ready to  pick out his victim or plan his approach for a predetermined victim. The exact situation will vary based on the practitioner's purposes. For example, someone who is looking to establish a relationship with a new victim might spend a great deal of time watching and learning all he can about a pool of potential victims, while someone who intends to get on someone's good side at his place of employment will have to work with the potential victim, along with his/her personality, demeanor, and vulnerability to manipulation. One thing to keep in mind is that not all practitioners of dark psychology simply pick out who they believe are the "easy" targets. Research has shown that a large number of narcissists actually enjoy the challenge of manipulating those "hard-to-gets" because having accomplished such a task only raises their own sense of superiority.

It is difficult to predict just how a dark psychology user chooses the victim to enact his/her strategies, but the observation and preparation period is when the practitioner will collect as much information on the target as possible before making a move. Of course, this is not always the case, especially in planned interactions that will take place on a one-time-only basis. But for the long-term victim, the practitioner must prepare carefully and devise a plan of attack that is likely to succeed if executed well.

What dark psychology cannot predict is how exactly the recipient is going to respond. In order to keep moving forward with an initial approach, the dark psychology user must be able to pick up on signals that broadcast how the victim is feeling and which give clues as to what he/she is thinking. The practiced manipulator will know what to look for in terms of body language and other verbal and physical clues to gauge how well he is doing and whether or not he needs to back off and try again later or find a new victim altogether.

The approach itself is meticulously thought through, and the demeanor and personality of the victim are often taken into account during the time when the practitioner is planning it. It is essential that the practitioner approaches in a way that is nonthreatening and friendly so as not to scare off the target. Once the interaction begins, the dark psychology user's goal is to present himself in a way that seems effortless and natural, while behind the scenes, he has put a great amount of thought and practice into this persona. His goal throughout this whole initial interaction is to gain rapport and form some kind of bond or trust so that he can open the door to further steps in his scheme. He looks for positive microexpressions and other body language cues, which will tell him whether or not the victim is comfortable or anxious. Microexpressions are very brief, telling expressions of the face which are far more subtle than the expressions we usually associate with people being happy, sad, or angry. They can last only a fraction of a second, yet if someone is watching closely, he can pick up on that brief signal which tells him a little bit more about how the subject is feeling.

Expressions of worry or discomfort will tell the practitioner that he needs to back off or use a different tactic, though it might be too late, and he may need to simply find another target and start over. These signals are numerous and vary widely based on personality and context, so let's look at an example to illustrate how a dark psychology user might read a target in order to get clues as to how he should proceed.

Annie is sitting alone in a park, reading a book. The manipulator—let's call him David—is nearby, watching and waiting to see if she has other obligations, such as meeting someone, looking after a child, etc. He waits long enough to gather that she is there by herself, simply enjoying the nice day and relaxing with a book. He decides this might be his perfect target.

He analyzes her clothes—very conservative, no makeup, with glasses. She didn't come out here with a lot of concern about dressing up or appearing effortfully attractive, though she is cute and doesn't need to try hard. He decides she isn't completely wrapped up in herself and may not be susceptible to a flirtatious approach. She will probably respond better to a very friendly, casual encounter that does not threaten to alter her day and her plan for it. However, she is also very attentive to her book, and she may be put off by someone interrupting her. Perhaps he should give the approach and, hopefully, the conversation follows a purpose and subject, say, the book she is reading. Perhaps he will tell her he is a teacher and appreciates a young person taking the time to read and enjoy a good book.

The dark psychology practitioner goes over his plan in his head and, when he feels prepared, he will make the approach.

Now, it's all about reading the reactions and behaviors of the subject. If Annie responds with a smile and friendly effect, then this gives him a signal that his approach is appropriate and that she is open to a friendly conversation. If she is short, not bothering to raise her eyes from the book, it might be a signal that she does not want to talk to anyone right now. The practitioner might move forward with his plan until he is rebuffed a second time, then back off.

In the situation where Annie seems amenable to a conversation, he sits down and begins speaking about his vocation, interest in books, etc. As he does this, he is careful to engage her and make eye contact, but not so much that he comes off creepy. He watches the subtle cues of her facial expressions. Furrowed brows might signal discomfort, while a smile that affects the skin around the eyes is genuine and signals that she is enjoying herself. The orientation of her body also tells him something. The more oriented her body is toward the speaker, the more engaged she is. If she remains upright and straight to the front or, worse, starts to turn away, it means she is anxious and uneasy about the interaction.

The practitioner will continue to act alongside these cues until he feels it is the right time to disengage, but he will do his best to "run into her again" or, if it feels right, ask specifically to meet up with her again, perhaps for a friendly cup of coffee.

Reading People From a Potential Victim's Point of View

If we take a look at Annie's point of view and see things from her angle, we can try to get a sense of what this encounter might feel like and how you yourself should handle yourself in such an encounter. The difficulty here, if the practitioner is good, is that there has yet to be any indication that this person is not who he says he is. Or is there? Here are some red flags to look out for when a stranger approaches you and tries to engage you, for whatever reason.

First of all, Annie may have noticed the presence of this man before if she had been paying attention. Remember how we discussed how David spent some looking around and observing potential targets? One of the first things you can do to protect yourself in public is to be aware of your surroundings. When Annie first gets to the park, she might look around and take note of the people who are there and what they are doing. A man alone staring at people is going to stand out and look weird next to a bunch of couples or families, playing with a dog, or kids walking around, eating ice cream. When this man approaches, she would have recognized him as someone acting oddly, so she would be careful to keep her distance and not relinquish any personal information. Also, she would probably not agree to a second meeting, especially if she paid attention to her gut feeling of unease.

Second, the man asking for your personal information may be a red flag. You should not give up personal information to strangers in an encounter like this. The man may very well be who he says he is, but you should still be careful if you decide to see him again. This very well could turn out to be a potential romantic relationship with someone who cares about the same things you do, but this kind of process takes time, and the dark psychology user is more likely to try and expedite the process through charm and clever lies. Be wary of someone who tries to expedite a friendly relationship with you right away.

Also, someone who is lying to you about his background or anything else will often shift his eyes away while he is thinking and coming up with the lie at the moment. Pay attention to his behavior, just like he is observing you, and look for signs that he is trying hard to think and fill in gaps in his story to  make himself sound more believable. Next, you can really throw a dark psychology user off guard by asking questions. Play his game against him and make him come up with good answers to personal questions and questions about his work, his pastimes, and where he lives. Nothing is off the table. If he is a genuine, honest person, this information will roll off the tongue, and you will probably get some kind of positive gut feeling that this person is not a threat. However, if you see this man fidgeting, looking away, or looking down at the ground, then it is likely he is trying hard to think of plausible answers, and you've knocked off his concentration.

In this situation, simply put up your guard, don't offer any relevant information about yourself or your life, and feel free to enact some of those signals mentioned above, which will broadcast disinterest. Make your conversation answers short to bring the interaction to an end, or ask directly that you be left alone as you just want to relax and read. These things will tell the dark psychology user that he is not going to get what he wants from you, and, hopefully, he will back off. If not, it's time to notify the authorities if he continues to follow you around. Call a friend to back you up where you are so that you do not lead him home. This is a worst-case scenario, and, hopefully, this never happens to you, but it is always good to have a plan for when something like this might occur.

Chapter 3: Manipulation Techniques

Manipulation techniques is a topic that covers a very wide range of tactics and practices, but we will cover some of the most commonly used and most insidious types of manipulation techniques here so that you have a better understanding of what is out there and how these individuals might work.

Three Modes of Persuasion

Aristotle outlined three modes of persuasion which continue to reflect how  people communicate with one another with the intention of persuading them to a similar point of view or opinion. Often, these three modes are combined in order to have the greatest effect, especially in the arena of someone giving a speech to many people at once. In order to convince as many different personalities as possible, the speaker employs arguments focused on the disciplines of logos, ethos, and pathos.

Logos is the mode of persuasion which has to do with a logical argument. The speaker centers his statements around a logical series of facts and evidence which is designed to lead the listener to a logical conclusion in line with his own position. This is often employed in political speeches and in many other areas where a person is trying to convince others to take action for his cause, whether that is a personal cause or something which he thinks will benefit a large number of people together. The arguments must be easy to follow and make the listeners feel as if the speaker is on the same level. It would be counterproductive to speak in terms that no one understands. The listeners might have a number of different reactions to this, including a feeling of being insulted, as well as alienated from the conversation. Persuasion in this form is considered manipulation under the loose definition of manipulation because you are employing a specific strategy in order to change people's minds and attempt to get them on your side. This strategy may also employ the use of only choosing specific information that supports your side of the argument while excluding any evidence of information that refutes it. This is one of the most common ploys when it comes to political campaigns, and two sides of the political divide might tell the same story completely differently based on what they choose to include and the type of "spin" they use to give listeners or readers a certain impression of the facts.

Another mode of persuasion, according to Artistotle, is the ethos route, which attempts to tap into listeners' emotions primarily as a way of convincing them to see the speaker's point of view. These modes can be enacted in whatever form available or preferable, such as writing in a newspaper or online, but we will stick with the visual of a speaker speaking to a group of people simply because it's a stronger illustration.

A speaker who chooses to employ an ethos mode of persuasion will often tell a story about his background or some other experience, which will work to get the listeners to feel sorry him or empathize with him in some way. Often, these experiences are tied into his current endeavor of gathering followers and convincing them that his plans are the best for accomplishing a certain goal. The speaker might do a bit of research in order to weed out what that community's struggles are in particular and then construct his speech around the emotional impact that this issue has raised in that community. By first arousing these emotions, the speaker can then turn to what he believes he can do to change it. When listeners' emotions are impacted and evoked, they are more willing to listen to potential solutions and propositions, which may or may not align with their political or established views. The focus moves to solve that specific problem. It is necessary here, also, that the people listening are firmly convinced of the speaker's honesty and genuine empathy for the people suffering or being hurt by whatever issue is being discussed. When the people feel that the speaker is not sincere, this could potentially completely derail any momentum the speaker may have had.

The final mode of persuasion offered by Aristotle is that of pathos. In the pathos mode, the focus is on the speaker or arguer himself and presenting the most perfect and admirable picture possible to the public. He will be presented as a man of great moral character, good experience, high social and political standing, and high accomplishment. The idea here is that the people will be so impressed by the individual himself that they will be convinced that whatever he is saying or fighting for is probably a good thing because he obviously knows what he's talking about. Granted, this particular mode is rarely used alone, but it is almost always utilized when other modes are in action. For example, the introduction of a speaker to the people listening before he gives a speech is a way to condition the crowd toward a particular view of the speaker getting ready to come on stage. The idea is to impress upon listeners, especially those who are not yet familiar with him, that this person is someone who deserves attention because of all these things that he has done, stands for, or represents.

Emotional Manipulation

Emotional manipulation techniques can be incredibly malicious in nature and have the potential to cause mental damage that the victim must often deal with for the rest of their lives. This is because, in the most difficult situation, the manipulator has taken the time and made an effort to develop a sense of trust and a strong relationship between himself and the victim. Alternatively, the manipulator may have fostered a somewhat healthy relationship before choosing to do something he knows would hurt his partner and himself in some way and then gradually develops a cycle of manipulation to hide what he's done through the exploitation of his partner's established love and trust. A classic example of this is the extramarital affair.

In other situations, we are talking about a short-term interaction which employs the victim's emotional capacity and vulnerability for only an amount of time required for the manipulator to acquire some kind of short-term reward. An example of this might be someone on the street looking for some extra cash who decides to tell a passerby an elaborate story of misfortune in order to guilt the person into giving over some cash or spare change. The interaction is very short-term, and once the goal is accomplished, the manipulator moves on to his next goal.

The range of emotional manipulation techniques and scenarios is vast, but we will be focusing on some of the major and most harmful situations in later chapters, which usually involve some degree of emotional manipulation. The key here is to define what we are talking about when we discuss emotional manipulation, and it is the technique which focuses on evoking very specific emotions or even cocktails of emotional responses in order to condition the victim to be more vulnerable and help the manipulator toward his ultimate goals, whether they are aware of it or not.

There are many techniques and specific tactics that fit under the umbrella term of emotional manipulation. One of these techniques is gaslighting, in which the victim is convinced, over time, to start to doubt their reality and become confused based on a manipulator's consistent and repetitive denial and subjugation of the accusations presented to him. This is most often manifested in the form of an abuser who takes harmful actions against a victim, but when asked to acknowledge the actions, often by the abused themselves, they will completely deny that they've done anything wrong and insist that the abuser is exaggerating or making stuff up. The victim in this scenario is gradually beaten and worn down emotionally, where, at first, she may have been strong and determined to get some kind of justice through an apology, but over time, she loses this strength and begins to doubt her own sanity. This can be an extremely mentally damaging scenario because it is inflicted over a long period of time, and the brain begins to form habits and whole new paradigms concerning the reality they thought they knew.

The point here is that this type of manipulation tactic would be very hard to accomplish without having first established a very strong emotional bond with the victim. The victim stays around or feels hope that they can improve their situation because they have developed some measure of love, trust, and respect, even if this abuser is not starting to take advantage of all this. The victim herself can often be in a state of denial for a long period of time, choosing to shoulder the blame for the abuse that is going on rather than accepting that the person she loves has turned into something else entirely or that she was mistaken about him in the first place. If you can imagine and place yourself in a scenario like this with someone in your own life whom you've grown to love and trust more than anyone else, you can probably start to see how someone could become emotionally vulnerable and susceptible to mind games, clinging to the hope that what she believed she has still exists.

Power Play and Dominance

Power plays and shows of dominance are often utilized in organizations where the manipulator must have the allegiance of his followers, employees, or colleagues. The arenas where this form of manipulation comes into play range from the parent-child dynamic to the dating scene at a dance club. Or, it could be in a team meeting at work with the person wanting to show his boss that he is the  most intelligent and hardworking and that he has the most leadership potential through the subjugation of the people he is working with. Power plays and shows of dominance can be utilized in the form of simple gestures and behaviors, such as the handshake where the dark psychology user's hand takes the palm-downward position. They can also be utilized as a part of grand schemes and long-term plans that work to influence and earn respect and admiration of groups of people, one person at a time.

The oldest and most primitive techniques aligned with this tactic involves physical presence and shows of strength. Put simply, the man with the strongest muscles and most intimidating stature might get a free pass to the competition for dominance as the male "alpha" of the group. This is a longstanding instinct, which had much use in the past when it was essential for people to stick together and also follow the same rules in order to get along and survive in a society. The same drives remain today; it is just the arenas that look a bit different.

Nowadays, you might see the example of dominance in a group of young kids who hang around each other, causing trouble and who tend to gravitate to the tallest boy, the best-looking boy, or the most charismatic. When there is a female or group of females around, it might be an unspoken assumption that the alpha gets to have the first choice before the others can make a move. This individual goes to great lengths in public to show and maintain his status among them, perhaps opting to encourage a fight that he can win in order to demand respect from anyone else who might challenge him.

But the dominance tactic can also be practiced in a much more nuanced way, such as in the corporate setting where different individuals vie for power and prominence. These people usually develop shrewd social skills that utilize manipulation in order to garner respect or even intimidation from his intended subjects. We will get into this in more detail in our chapter on workplace manipulation.

Charm and Flattery/Mirroring

Another major strategy we will introduce here involves playing on people's sense of vanity and self-awareness through the use of flattery, charm, and personality mirroring.

The saying "flattery will get you anywhere" is a pretty good summation of what's  going on when a person decides to manipulate another through the use of well-timed and effective flattery. The goal is not to overwhelm the victim, who might be suspicious of the motive. The goal is to be convincing and sincere so that she believes that the manipulator is truly taken with her in some way, be it purely physical or based on intelligence. The most basic and simple form of flattery might be to compliment a woman's smile, her dress, her makeup, and things like that. This might be used as one of the initial approach statements in order to warm up a victim for what is coming next. Granted, the manipulator has to be aware of his victims and be pretty good at gauging whether he will be successful with a certain victim or not. Some people, usually the more experienced and cynical types, will immediately turn to suspicion when someone begins using flattery on them. This is probably because they've been taken advantage of before.

This is where we can impress again the importance of the manipulator's first steps of observation of potential victims. He is going to zero in on the young, naïve individual before the stern-looking hard-ass in the corner by herself. At a party or in a public setting where there is alcohol, the abuser may pick up on the presence of young women who are having a good time flirting with lots of different men. These women may be the most susceptible to manipulation and the most affected by tactics of flattery and charm in order to get into a conversation with the dark psychology user who may then be able to move forward with his intents.

Charm is all about apparent sincerity and entertainment. A man with a good sense of humor and conversation skills will be more capable of entertaining a victim, and the longer the abuser can keep a person engaged, the more likely he is to be successful in moving toward getting what he wants. The individual with a high degree of skill in the charm and flattery categories may be able to conjure attraction to him within the victim, further conditioning her to his will.

Lastly, mirroring comes into play when a manipulator is trying to make a target feel comfortable enough to release information that might be useful to the abuser. This often occurs in situations where an individual is trying to ingratiate himself to another who is in a position of power over him. The intent behind this behavior might be to get "in" with the people who make the decisions in order to move up the ladder, or else he might be trying to protect himself from getting on this person's bad side. This type of situation is often parodied in movies where the detective or investigator needs to infiltrate a building or a hideout, and he must work to mirror the people he comes into contact with in order to avoid arousing suspicion.

Mirroring involves simply observing the target closely and mirroring back the little mannerisms and aspects of the target's personality back to him so that he feels comfortable. This is one way in which dark psychology takes into account the basic human behaviors and tendencies, which underlie the way we all interact and form impressions of one another. A lot of these mechanisms in action happen under the radar, in the subconscious. We all react more positively in situations where we are dealing with people who are similar to us compared to the people who seem different in some way.

And it is often not just the feeling of comfort that is being affected but the established prejudices or formed opinions, having been established through our families or other experiences, which are triggered when we meet someone new. For example, if we had been brought up in a family of very devout Catholics and, for the first time, we meet someone from a different country who worships a different god, we may feel much more uneasy and unsure of the interaction compared to meeting someone from our own church, for example. This is an automatic sensation in most cases and is rooted in the evolutionary imperative that "different" often means danger, and "similar" signals comfort and safety.

In our next chapter, we will dig a little bit deeper into the mechanisms and strategies that play out in situations of emotional manipulation at work.

Chapter 4: Emotional Manipulation

In this chapter, we will work from the small-scale, short-term forms and scenarios of manipulation and move up to the most insidious, long-term examples of dark psychology utilizing human emotions.

Short-Term Manipulation

As we have illustrated in the last chapter, the example of a street beggar telling an emotional story to get a few bucks from a stranger is one of the simplest forms of emotional manipulation. The abuser has a short-term goal and plays upon one of the people's most common social tendencies in order to get what he wants. And then the interaction is over. This is a tactic that can be repeated over and over with somewhat similar results, involving a lot of different people simply because the universal human emotion of guilt and the tendency of empathy between human beings are relatively constant across a population. The only requirement for success in such a situation is for the story to be believed by the targets, and that elicits the desired emotional response.

Numerous situations reflect this same type of mode of short-term manipulation for the sake of simple, short-term goals, often in the form of money. Emotional reactions can be amped up or down, perhaps through the involvement of other people being affected, like children. A person who comes to a stranger's door asking for help might mention that his children are sitting in a car without dinner might work to elicit a stronger emotional response.

Other much more malicious intents might prey upon similar emotional responses, but the consequences of success on the part of the manipulator are much more catastrophic. For example, the serial killer Ted Bundy was famous for eliciting the help of young, naïve women through a mixture of charm and conjuring feelings of pity, mixed with a sense of urgency. He did this by wearing a cast and, in the prime moment when the victim was in view, he would fumble with a pile of books or something else as if he was trying to get them in his car and was having trouble doing it by himself. The young women would notice this and go over and offer to help, seeing that this man was having trouble. It didn't hurt that Bundy was a good-looking man, and women were often immediately enamored of him when they saw them. This immediate charm mixed with pity and a willingness to help someone in need was the perfect setting for Bundy to move in on the opportunity, usually knocking the victim unconscious before loading them in the car toward their doom.

Long-Term Manipulation

When we move into the more long-term practice of emotional manipulation tactics, we start to zero in on the necessity for the abuser to establish trust and love before enacting his manipulative intents. This could happen on the scale of a one-night stand, or the manipulator could put a plan into action that will last weeks, months, or even years. His goals might be anything from sex and money to emotional support for his own troubled and needy mind. On top of the tactics of deceit as demonstrated in the short-term situation, the abuser must be able to take on a completely different personality if the intent is to lure the target into a potential relationship, romantic or otherwise. The manipulator's intent must remain hidden, so he must conjure an alternative intention which will serve as the motivating factor for the interaction and subsequent relationship. Those personality types of dark triad often become particularly skilled in this area out of necessity and a complete lack of compassion or remorse for having duped a victim and hurt them emotionally. The abusers on the spectrum of deviant personalities, who regularly employ emotionally manipulative tactics in order to get what they want from people, range in intelligence from the highly intelligent, meticulous planner to the simple-minded, anomalistically motivated abuser. Each person on this spectrum of abusers is looking for something or a group of rewards, which correspond to some need or desire. One may be purely motivated by sex, another by emotional siphoning and control, and another by the challenge of the game. Some abusers harbor feelings of hatred and frustration and wish to inflict harm on a target because the one responsible for his pain is either dead or unavailable in some way. Emotional manipulation often becomes a necessity for someone who has not developed normally, perhaps emotionally or sexually or in the arena of social skills and, therefore, cannot form healthy relationships in "normal" ways.

Those abusers who manage long-term emotional manipulation usually have some  degree of prowess in the form of social skills or a high degree of intelligence, even if the underlying capacity for empathy, compassion, and relatability are completely lacking. They know that what they have to work with personally is not going to get them where they need to be, so the compulsion to manipulate and entice another person through fabricated feelings is so strong that they practice and learn to put the time and effort into their craft so that they are essentially "experts" in their fields.

There are also those who practice manipulation without employing study or research in order to hone these skills. These skills are part of a personality that is devoid of any capacity even to recognize that their behaviors are deviant and hurtful. These are natural manipulators who find themselves having a lot of trouble operating in the world and are much more susceptible to actively turn toward criminal activity out of frustration or anger. They are the rapists, the hired killers, the employees of those criminal actions that skip the manipulation component entirely and take what they want by force. What emotional manipulation skills they acquire are taught to them through experience or a specific teacher to utilize these skills for their specific tasks, but this will not go very far (long-term) simply because of being completely unnatural and their anathema to their innate natures.

The final topic under emotional manipulation is the long-term emotional corrosion of an abuser whose mentality changes over time through some kind of long-term influence. These abusers often bring others down with them in the form of immediate family members or close friends. These are the domestic abuse cases where a couple seemed to have a perfectly normal and happy relationship until something changed in the dynamic or lifestyle, and the relationship began to degrade. Influential factors might include things like gradual addiction to alcohol, being laid off at work, other forms of shared financial difficulty, a traumatic experience that is not processed in a way that is healthy or is faced with denial, or a sudden betrayal of trust that prompts long-lasting grudges and resentment. All of these factors may contribute to the formation of a relentless emotional cycle of manipulation and abuse, where the abuser turns all of those negative feelings and begins to project them outward, either as a weapon or as a way to avoid dealing with them himself.

In a previous example, we talked about the tactic of stringing along a victim while the abuser turns to other sources of comfort or other endeavors while keeping just enough contact in place so that the victim believes he will come back and that the estrangement is just temporary. After this experiment, the abuser might realize that this tactic actually adds to the level of attachment and desperation in the victim, thereby offering him a degree of control, which is often quite intoxicating. The abuser will continue this cycle as he sees how far he can go without prompting the victim to give up on the hope and attachment she feels.

An alternative situation is that of the jealous lover who plays mind games and demeans the victim into a place where they do not feel they deserve to have interaction with any other human beings at all, thus securing an environment of control over the victim for the abuser. The abuser will degrade the victim's self-confidence and sense of self-worth until they are no more than husks of the person they used to be.

When the abuser can reach this point, he has successfully formed in his mind the ideal victim because she has completely lost the will to fight for herself or stand up for her mental well-being. Emotionally manipulative tactics become much easier, and the abuser will only lose more and more of whatever sense of guilt or conscience he might have had once, as this way of life and dominance become easier and more like routine. He might employ tactics of yelling and intimidation to maintain this sense of control; he might punish the victim for what he calls infractions whenever the victim ventures out of his established expectations for her.

This type of situation and state of emotional degradation does not happen overnight, as we've discussed. This form of long-term abuse is a situation that gains gradual traction and momentum until it seems the train cannot be stopped. It is often baffling to friends and loved ones when a marriage or relationship that once seemed healthy goes downhill this way, but it is important to remember that no one is immune to something like this happening to them. In each situation, there is a complex set of factors and events that gradually contribute to the destruction of people's emotional strength, and eventual degradation of the bond of love and trust and respect often follows. We will discuss the importance of self-esteem in the next chapter.

Chapter 5: The Importance of Self-Esteem

Emotional manipulation preys on the subject's self-esteem in a lot of situations. Especially when it comes to women, self-esteem can be influenced and manipulated through social ideal comparative tactics, as well as personal attacks based on the subject's feelings of validation and value as a woman.

The "Ideal Woman"

In modern-day culture, especially in America, women are bombarded with a nonstop influx of images and impressions that give them a superficial idea of what or how a woman should look, feel, and act like. Often, this "ideal woman" is oblivious  to the position of confidence and self-worth that comes from inside one's self rather than the validation from others—mostly men. These women are raised in a social and popular environment that encourages competition with other women for the attention of men. Social media, magazine images, and advertisements in all its forms are all complicit in the form of emotional manipulation on a broad scale. They manipulate women's minds with the goal of trading money for self-esteem builders. But in order to be convinced to make this trade, women need to be convinced that who or what they are is not good enough. But—if they just buy this magazine with new sex tips or advice for how to dress or follow this

Instagram star who will show you how to be really sexy and give you something emulate—then just maybe, with enough time and attention, you can be good enough! This is a general message perpetuated over time and has now taken over a large part of the mental space that kids and young adults spend their time mired in every single day.

But it's important to note that men are not immune to these efforts. Images and social media pages filled with information about how to get the perfect body, how to get the women to fall in love with them, or how to juggle multiple sex partners are also all over the place. Porn can shape a young mind's idea of what sex is supposed to be like and how they are supposed to act and feel and all the things that a healthy human being would have learned through personal experience and establishing his or her own identity without such superficial outside influence. However, it is nearly impossible nowadays to be engaged with the world without being inundated with such influences, and this leads to this chapter's topic on the importance of self-esteem.

Self-esteem can be targeted by advertisements, social media, and other forms of social influence in individuals as young as 9 and 10 years old. We know this because research has shown through surveys that many girls start dieting and doing things to alter their appearances and become more socially acceptable around this time in their lives. That is a staggering realization to take in. And the pressure and influence only get stronger as we grow older and are faced with new ideas rehashed to fit our paradigms as we age, adopt new careers, and face marriage, family, etc. These images follow us around for our entire lives, so how can you foster your own sense of identity and build your self-esteem? The answers will be a little different for each individual, but the importance of addressing this issue extends to creating a form of defense against those who prey on emotional vulnerability.

One of the most efficient ways you might begin this process is to limit your exposure to social media and any media to which you compare yourself, whether consciously or subconsciously. This can be damaging on a level that we do not even recognize until we are in those moments when we are deeply displeased or  even in despair about some aspect of ourselves which we perceive others might deem unappealing or not good enough in some way. It is important to build up your own sense of self and identity, or else it becomes easy for advertisers to hijack who you believe you are and what you should be. A dark psychology user will be able to pick up on someone with exceptionally low self-esteem, especially if he is skilled in his tactics. There are certain unconscious signals that we give off when our confidence is low, and we feel self-conscious. These are indicators of a person with low self-esteem. Body language such as crossed arms and legs and a lack of eye contact, bad posture, and wide eyes that dart around without a point of concentration all signal self-consciousness and nervousness. These are like sending a signal directly to the dark psychology user, which says, "I am easy prey." The trick is to manage these body language signals and adjust them even if you are not feeling particularly confident. You can mask yourself and your unease to ward off predatory types while in pubic. Alternatively, figure out what it is you need in public or at work function or parties that will help boost your confidence and lessen your self-consciousness. Perhaps sticking close to a friend would help you feel secure or talking to someone who seems to have good social skills to teach you how to mingle and talk confidently. The worst thing you could do in a public situation is to go off alone while broadcasting your insecurity. Do not do anything to make it easier for manipulators to get to you if possible.

Self-confidence and building self-esteem on the inside rather than masking insecurity is, of course, the preferable route to building a strong defense against dark psychology users. This route is not usually easy and will look different for each individual. However, we will offer some tips and suggestions for you to try and see if they don't help you along.

Build Self-Esteem Through Meditation

First of all, set aside time each day for a brief meditation. Yes, I said meditation. If you know nothing about meditation, don't worry. There is a lot of convoluted information out there about the practice, but the core of meditation and its practice is actually quite simple. To begin, we suggest you set aside just 10 to 20 minutes a day to be alone in a quiet place. The object of this time is to pull you away from your daily distractions in order to address that place inside of you which is insecure or less confident than the person you work hard to portray to others. You must take a look inside yourself and determine the source of your insecurity in order to address it meaningfully. If you are a total beginner with meditation, practice by simply paying attention to your breath as you breathe deeply throughout the course of your time set aside for meditation. Try to center your thoughts in the present and on your breath, and when you catch your thoughts wandering, gently redirect your focus. Don't worry about clearing your thoughts like erasing a blackboard; it will be impossible to just get rid of your thinking mind, and failing will just make you more frustrated with the process.

Let your mind wander if it wants to—and it probably will for the first few sessions—but then just bring your focus back to your breath, like a reminder now and again. Once you feel comfortable with this simple concept of meditation, try to move on to a session when you pinpoint the things about yourself from which you draw strength. Focus on the strengths rather than the weaknesses, and this will be the focus of your new meditation. What can you use to build your self-confidence? Are you good at your job? Are you hood at being a spouse or partner? Are you good at a certain craft or hobby? Whatever is, you want to re-establish for yourself that these pastimes have value and that they make you unique. They should have more weight than the frivolous preoccupations most people have with physical appearance and impressions that come from superficial values, such as money, possessions, and position at work. It's not a bad thing to be proud of these aspects of your life if you have them, but they will never fulfill the real person inside who is asking for more in life. You cannot derive happiness and confidence purely from the influence of others; it is something you must cultivate within yourself. Make sure you are following your own path, with your own goals waiting for you at the end. Reaching such goals will renew your life and self-esteem.

Take Care of Your Health and Body

Another thing that will help you build self-esteem is to take better care of your body. The idea here is not to lose weight to become attractive to other people; it is to improve your health and boost your sense of overall wellbeing and confidence. Do it for yourself first and foremost, not to look good for other people. You might see areas of improvement, such as the way you eat or your exercise habits. Try to find something in the exercise realm that you genuinely enjoy so that the exercise does not just feel like an obligation. Doing this will make sure that you don't give up early on, out of boredom. In addition, finding an exercise that involves being outside will do a lot for your mood overall, which is always good. If you find that you often suffer from bouts of anxiety or even depression, sunlight, and fresh air are proven remedies that can help you get back on track and find yourself and your confidence again.

Build a Support System

Another route to building self-confidence and self-esteem is to keep those who build you up close and get rid of those bad influences in your life, which you know bring you down. This can be a tricky one, as sometimes bad influences come in the form of close friends or family members. To figure out if there is something that needs attention in this category, you might consider sitting down and writing out a journal entry or some kind of list, which will help you closely consider your relationships and the influence they have on your life. Who are your best friends? How do they make you feel? Do they influence you toward unhealthy habits? Who makes you feel good, and who makes you feel bad? Is your family supportive? Do you keep close contact with those who build you up? Pay attention to how you will honestly answer these questions. Some of the answers might be difficult realizations, but this could be one of the most important steps you can take toward building yourself anew as a self-sustaining and more confident person. Another thing to look for is whether or not you are actually leaning on a poor influence, whether it's about money or emotional support. When we use others as a crutch, even if they are willing to offer the support, we undermine our self-confidence in a big way. Over time, we begin to accept that we can't do anything on our own, and this becomes ingrained in our psyches and manifests as insecurity. A lot of the time, we convince ourselves that we are actually more dependent on some source of support than we actually are just because it's comfortable. Keeping in mind that there is a difference between using someone as a crutch and utilizing genuinely needed support, try to find a path toward independence from whatever is holding you back. Perhaps you are holding on to an old romantic relationship with someone simply because you are afraid of being alone, or you are holding on to an old friendship that doesn't really help you as a person and is actually intoxicating as an influence toward unhealthy ways of thinking or behavior. Whatever your situation is, it is up to you to improve it in order to progress toward your goals of becoming a more confident and independent person.

Finally, once you've pinpointed your sources of self-esteem, take steps toward strengthening those relationships, which you know help build you up as a person. If you have friends who feel good to be around in a genuine, healthy way, then put some effort into making time for them each week so that you can benefit from this positive influence. Something that might help a lot is to have an open discussion with this friend or group of friends about what you are trying to do in your life and how you want to work toward building self-esteem. These people are probably the ones who know you better than anyone else, so they may have some valuable input for you in terms of who they perceive you to be and what they feel are areas where you seem to struggle and which you may not have noticed before. These positive relationships may be family instead of friends, or perhaps even your own partner whom you haven't had a lot of time for recently. When we make time to have genuine face-to-face interactions with the people who hold value in our lives, we get a lot more out of the experience than if we are constantly distracting ourselves alone or in groups with media and other things that keep the personal interactions from happening. This often turns into a safe place that chases away the anxiety of having to open up to other people, but it will lead to nowhere but isolation, loneliness, and emptiness. Truly positive relationships that help you build yourself up as a person are built on the foundation of being a safe, open, and honest place to talk about the things that are not so comfortable or happy or superficial. People need to be able to talk about their problems and insecurities, so do your best to get past that initial anxiety about upsetting the tranquil, superficial waters, and take a risk with the ones you truly trust, love, and respect. When this happens, you are likely to find that your friends, who are positive influences to you, or group of loved ones have the same craving as you and will appreciate the opportunity to open up a new outlet for interaction and relationship. Spend some time listening to the concerns and problems of your friends as well. Encourage a relationship where there's free communication in a way that is nonjudgmental. We are struggling with something, so be as supportive to your friends as they have been for you. Relationships built on trust will be a huge asset as you change certain things about your life in order to build self-confidence and self-esteem.

Chapter 6: Workplace Manipulation

Workplace manipulation takes many forms, so we will look at some examples from different people's points of view.

Using Manipulation to Climb the Corporate Ladder

Most often, workplace manipulation is about building one's own prestige within  the environment for the sake of pursuing self-centered goals. But there are lots of different nuanced forms of manipulation that take place in the office and other workplace environments, which are not necessarily consciously undertaken. A lot of the time, it boils down to people's sense of importance when it comes to how others view them and what their positions are within the company. Let's illustrate something like this that might be going on inside the boardroom meeting of higherups within a company.

We'll say that this company is pretty sizeable and competitive within its industry with lots of people working on the upper management side as the company expands and works to manage its locations. Each individual here holds some level of power over certain areas and branches of the company, but there is room for people to move up as the business continues to do well and positions open up in order to manage more and more property. You can bet that this upward mobility currently present within the company is one of the primary thoughts on these people's minds as they interact with their bosses and conceive ideas for growth in an effort to impress those who are in charge and those who make company-wide decisions. This is an area where politics may come into play and where manipulation tactics related to politics are working from both sides. A top executive might push himself forward by offering ideas and refuting the ideas of others in order to make himself look like the smartest one in the room. Such actions might prompt other people in the room to form alliances against him in order to tear him down or to make room for themselves.

Using Manipulation to Defend One's Position

On the flip side, those in the top positions will feel a need and desire to hold onto power through demonstrations of dominance and domineering tactics even when they are not entirely applicable or necessary in order to prove the point of his/her seniority and position. Now, of course, this doesn't apply to every person in a place of power within a company, but there is certainly an argument to be made that those instincts which prompt people to exert themselves in order to maintain control of a population would be triggered in a position of power. At these positions, the stakes become higher and blame is often placed on those at the top of a company. Therefore, actions of manipulation might stem from fear, which is a very strong motivator toward actions and decisions that may not be entirely ethical but rather a desperate attempt to hang on to power and influence and make sure no one crosses him/her in his/her decisions. People who make it to the top of a prestigious company often let this kind of position and power go to their heads in different ways, manifesting as a domineering presence that must be obeyed and bowed to for fear of being cut out of the game entirely. This kind of dominating presence is often fueled by a growing desire linked with greed and power-hungry cravings, which only manifest once the individual has had a taste of the power that seems to win them such prizes. There is a whole area of research surrounding the phenomenon and effects of power on the individual psyche, but corruption is a common consequence.

We've seen this unfold all over the news in America where people at the highest echelons of power seem to hit a point somewhere along the line where they no longer make business decisions that involve the interests of the people responsible for holding the company up, but which seem solely concerned with the unstoppable growth and dominance of the company within its industry. This is, after all, one of the most important aspects of working and managing a company that is ingrained in employees from the moment they start working. The capitalist economy is all about growth and economic dominance. The leaders consider themselves ultimately responsible for this aspect of the business and often make decisions that minimize the importance of those at the bottom while doing whatever it takes to increase the profits coming in. The mode of control for individuals in these positions is often to practice manipulation techniques.

In order to make sure everyone within the company is doing their jobs and keeping nothing in their minds except perfect operation, the people in power must persuade and charm his underlings so as to convince them that their work is thoroughly appreciated and vital to the successful operation of the company. This is done through lots of attention to the business statement of purpose and how the company improves society and offers something of value to everyone involved and to all customers helping to keep the company going. These value statements often seem completely altruistic in nature, as if the ultimate aim of the company is to help this specific niche of human individuals, and this goal goes far beyond simple monetary concerns as the primary objective. In this way, workers can be inspired to do their jobs to the best of their ability with the belief system that they are working for the people who are buying their products, and not just to boost the income of the people who are in charge and running the company from the top. This is a form of internal and nonpersonal manipulation, with decisions and actions being taken from the top which then spread throughout the company through different modes of communication and dissemination of information through such individuals as middle management in order to get to those on the lowest "rung" of the corporate ladder. As this is done, it soon becomes part of the paradigm of working there, and it becomes an essential part of the public identity of that company.

This all seems sinister on the face of it, but it is all about the balance that is demanded from a market economy between filling a need within society and also building up the business so that it becomes dominant in the industry and remains successful and sustainable. There is nothing wrong with maintaining a proper balance between these two concerns, but, all too often, the scales start to tip toward economic dominance within an industry and the greed of those in power. This movement prompts manipulation as a necessity to maintain the façade of the balance, which may or may not have existed at the outset.

Now, let's scale down a bit and talk about how an individual employee might utilize tactics of manipulation in order to build himself up above everyone else. There is a tendency within groups of human beings that is quite effective in this context. For example, a boss assigns a group of employees to work as a team on a certain project. They are to meet and  brainstorm ideas to come up with a detailed plan on how to proceed. An employee who has his sights set on climbing up the ladder can use this situation to his advantage if he plays it right.

The person in group meetings who talks the loudest and is the most charismatic will have an instinctively more profound effect on the minds of those around him compared to the one who sits back in the corner or talks in a quieter tone of voice and affect. Even if this quieter individual has the better ideas, the group will tend to lean toward the one with much more confidence, and this is something that is ingrained within us as human beings, in relation to the establishment of an alpha or leader, which goes back to the first manifestations of human society on earth. We can't get away from the tendencies tied to human nature, though we can work to be conscious of when someone is using this as a part of manipulative tactics. Without thinking about it, however, the team will automatically start to lean toward this confidence, charismatic voice in the room, and, ultimately, this individual will use this phenomenon as a way to make himself seem like the prominent voice of leadership from the perspective of his boss—and this is the ultimate goal.

Unfortunately, because of this phenomenon, many bad decisions are often made without the realization that they were not the best ideas until it is too late. The fact that this is an often subconscious mechanism of human nature means it is not always something that people realize is happening to them at the moment when they are making those crucial decisions.

Using Manipulation to Gain Power Over Colleagues

Another manipulation tactic that people often see in the workplace is that which works to belittle and undermine others as a means to make themselves feel better or superior in their positions. The irony is that, often, people who enact this kind of insidious manipulation in the workplace do not hold positions of power above those they demean. This can actually be one of the primary drivers for someone to behave this way against other people. Especially men who feel that they are not in the position that is commensurate with what they feel they deserve will be susceptible to the temptation to act out their frustration and take it out on others with whom they interact on a daily basis. This is simply convenient for them because of the ease of access and their availability to become easy prey. The manipulator in this context will quickly learn who in their environment would make good targets. In other words, these are people who are unlikely to fight back or defend themselves. Here, we return to the concepts we've discussed in previous chapters about how the manipulator will choose his prey. Will he go after the diminutive and weak-willed, self-conscious young woman who has just started at the company or the confident woman who doesn't take crap from anyone? The answer should be obvious. Therefore, it is essential that those in the environment look out for one another when it comes to defending against manipulation in the workplace.

Unfortunately, people do not always take it upon themselves to look out for one another in an increasingly individualistic society that operates on an everyone-for-himself basis. In addition, the manipulator may be smart enough to know that he must operate in a way that is not obvious to the other coworkers around him. He will pinpoint and target a single individual and take opportunities when he can, perhaps even convincing the target to take on extra workloads. The effect here would be that the manipulator feels a sense of power that is false but nevertheless comforting. The manipulative tactics utilized in this context are most often that of belittling and undermining the already low-confidence level of the target. The target will start to feel as if she has no choice as she is persistently told that she needs to get better at her job and take on more responsibility in order to be noticed. Alternatively, the manipulator might employ tactics that focus on engaging the target's good-natured feelings and tendencies. These would include feeling sorry for him and like she should help him, that he is genuinely in need of support and assistance, and that she should feel guilty for not wanting to help him. These feelings can be evoked through direct confrontation with the manipulator as he drops subtle cues to trigger these emotions. The effect may not take place right away, but most of the most malicious dark psychology tactics begin with the planting of simple, unnoticed seeds of doubt and emotional manipulation, which grow over time.

In this way, workplace manipulation can work just as effectively as manipulation situations at home because a person often spends almost as much time at the office working as they do at home relaxing. The psychic effects of workplace manipulation can be just as harmful and can make the target feel trapped. Not everyone feels they have the capability to just pick up and leave a job, especially if they have become invested in their careers. People put up with unpleasant interactions at work every day for the sake of responsibility for the wellbeing of their families. Unhappiness and dissatisfaction in the workplace can lead to others viewing you as a way to alleviate their own stress through covert abuse and emotional manipulation. On the flip side, those who feel as if they are under a large amount of stress may become the perpetrators of such workplace abuse as a way to alleviate their stress and not even realize they are turning into this kind of person. We all do what we can, sometimes unconsciously, to alleviate stress from whatever source. These mechanisms can happen automatically and without conscious thought—just like when something happens, and we get suddenly very frustrated and angry. We seem unable to control the feelings that arise and, if we are not careful, may form habits of reaction in these situations which are harmful, either to ourselves or those around us. It is important that people do not underestimate the psychological effects of their stress and their reactions to that stress on other people, most often on the people they love the most.

Sometimes, all it takes is for someone to point out to the abuser that his behavior is out of line. He may not realize the extent to which he has let his automatic reactions to stress get out of hand. If this tactic does not work, then it may be necessary to notify a manager or supervisor in order to have the behavior addressed. If you find yourself the target of workplace manipulation and abuse and cannot successfully address it yourself, then you need to seek out help and support in order to make the behavior stop. Perhaps you can move departments or surround yourself with a different team. Your boss or supervisor should take this kind of thing seriously and take steps to alleviate the effects of such abuse and put a stop to the abuse itself. Do not underestimate the long-term effects of just taking it upon yourself to put up with it and deal with it. A lot of people start out thinking they are too strong to be affected by long-term abuse, but the human psyche only has so much it can put up with before it starts to give in. Enlist the help of those you trust to help you navigate the situation.

Chapter 7: Manipulative Partners

One of the most malicious and harmful forms of manipulation happens in the place that most of us believe are the most comfortable and safest to spend our time—inside your own home.

But the truth is, people live out years and even decades of their lives under the  influence of a manipulative partner. We read stories and headlines all the time about the manipulation that can happen inside the home and how sometimes it can lead to physical altercations, abuse, and even spousal homicide. The manipulation that occurs inside the home between partners employ the most powerful and influential forms of emotional manipulation in existence, and it works on a scale that tampers with the very souls and hearts of the targets.

When a form of manipulation by a partner is very successful, it is because the manipulator has been able to pinpoint exactly where the partner is most vulnerable emotionally. This area of vulnerability will be different in each person, and, certainly, there are those who are much more manipulatable than others of a stronger constitution and higher emotional intelligence. We will focus on some of the most common emotional strategies employed by manipulators in the home.

Flattery and Superficial Charm

Superficial relationships employ superficial pleasures and techniques. These are the kinds of relationships that might start through an initial sexual encounter and which sustains itself based purely on the initial excitement and pleasure coming from an exciting new affair, extramarital or otherwise. Predators in this arena often juggle multiple partners at the same time and become quite talented at compartmentalizing each interaction and keeping them separate from each other. This is vital to a successful manipulative tactic in this context because he, most often, will employ excessive charm and flattery in order to put the target in a place psychologically where she is most susceptible. As with all of the most skilled dark psychology users, the practitioner will have picked out his target specific to his intentions and tactics. Those women who spend all of their time on their looks and making themselves public on social media are often the most susceptible to flattery and superficial charm tactics. They enjoy the attention and compliments, and they often form a kind of addiction to this attention, using it as a way to sustain themselves and their self-esteem. When they don't get this attention, their esteem and confidence might plummet to a place where they become desperate, often utilizing sexual influence in order to garner the attention and admiration they've developed such a need for.

This type of tactic can be quite economical for the manipulator because talk is cheap. When a person's self-esteem and trust stem simply from a steady influx of flattery and charm, that person can be pretty easy to string along for a decent amount of time. If there is financial support coming in as well, then the target can be quite satisfied to turn a blind eye to behaviors that might be the antithesis to the things she is hearing from her partner.

Superficial means of control and manipulation are effective for short-term gain, but the effects of this behavior often catch up to the manipulator in some way or another. The targets of such manipulation are also susceptible to being stolen away, as the emotional attachment present in deeper types of emotional manipulation do not take hold in the same way regarding this superficial charm-based manipulation. Anyone who comes along with more material wealth and steady use of charm and flattery may ignite a desire to switch gears, stemming from a mentality that the "grass may be greener on the other side." Without the bond of love or trust holding her back, this might be an easy choice to take. When this situation arises, it is common for the manipulator to act out in the way of violent or abusive behavior in order to keep his targets "in line." Jealousy and the need for control and dominance often accompany the desire to gather "trophies" through superficial manipulation, and the prize of maintaining control over his prey is not grounded in a deep, fulfilling relationship, but rather the status that comes along with "owning" a woman.

Women are just as capable of stringing along a man, perhaps through a much more powerful persuasion tactic of sex and desire. Those men who are obviously drawn to and dominated by the pursuit of women are easy targets for predatory women of this type. It is easy to pick out these types of men in a crowd or to simply attract them through flirtation. Men can be susceptible to letting down their guards emotionally when they choose to prioritize sex in a relationship. In order to support these desires and fool themselves into thinking they are being fulfilled on a deeper level, they can buy in all sorts of psychological manipulative techniques, which work to convince the target that there are real love and respect within the relationship. Women who are skilled in this type of manipulation will be quite insidious in their mixture of tactics, turning the tables and inciting guilt  when they see the opportunity to make their target feel bad for something they did. They can ignite their partner's sense of protecting what's theirs and even encourage the partner to act unethically on the predator's behalf, all in the name of a false claim of love.

Gradual Emotional Breakdown

This form of psychological manipulation and abuse adheres to a principle of kicking the target while she's down. Over time, the target is told over and over again that she is not good enough in some way. Once the manipulator figures out what is most painful to the victim, he may use this as his weapon in this regard. For example, if the target feels self-conscious about her physical appearance, this becomes the abuser's subject of torture, and he will use the weapon often, especially if he sees it effectively breaking down the mental strength and composure of the victim. Doing this offers an unchallenged level of control and influence over the victim, and, once there, the abuser will continue to exercise the tactic in order to keep her in that low place. This kind of emotional abuse is often accompanied by physical abuse, as well. The target who has been worn down through emotional abuse will also be unable to defend herself effectively, as the will to live itself is broken down alongside any sense of self-confidence or identity. The reward for this type of abuse works differently for the abuser in a lot of these cases. He is not usually trying to gain something from the victim but is rather releasing the frustration, anger, or depression that he feels himself and is unable to deal with. He passes along this pain in order to alleviate himself of some of the stress and pressure in some way, often functioning in complete denial of his actions as a way to live with himself as he continues this behavior.

Most of the time, there is no winner in these unfortunate circumstances. Both parties are spiraling downward. The longer this behavior continues, the more obscure the way out becomes. Other factors complicate this situation, such as kids and financial status. Women may feel trapped within an abusive relationship because they depend on the partner for financial support or other kinds of support. There might also be the threat of physical harm to the children should the victim take any action toward getting out of the situation, to get either her children or herself away. At this point, the abuser is driven by the simple and basic drive to possess and control without any concern as to what he is actually gaining out of the situation. This feeling will often persist in situations where the abuser has lost control in all other aspects of his life or in situations where he was brought up in a similar environment and understands no alternative way to live and operate in relation to other people.

Attachment and the Fear of Loss

Another type of manipulation in romantic relationships is one that preys on a person's fear of loss and sense of attachment or addiction to the manipulator. This can be one of the most effective when it comes to long-term manipulation because of the strength of the target's fear and aversion to loss or doing anything to jeopardize losing possession. Many people don't think of themselves as being addicted to possession, but the truth is that when a person develops a relationship with another human being, part of that presence is a formed attachment that receives reinforcement the longer he/she stays with that partner. Love can be gained and lost over time, but the attachment and habitual presence of a partner can be something that is very hard to overcome, and this is what makes the loss of a loved one or partner so difficult to manage, even if there has been an estrangement in terms of romantic love or affection.

The manipulator who chooses this path is often much more intellectually involved with the process than someone who chooses a different, more emotionally, and superficially based tactics, such as the situations discussed above. This kind of manipulation takes a bit of forethought and planning as well as a good sense of timing and ability to read a potential target and victim.

A lot of success in this particular tactic depends on the nature and personality of the victim. That is why choosing a victim who is susceptible to being controlled and manipulated in this way is an important first step should the manipulator have the opportunity to choose. Alternatively, this type of manipulation might manifest later on as changes take place in the relationship and the more dominant partner decides to take advantage of this trait in order to maintain control or gain access to some different type of reward. Once this vulnerability is known to the abuser, it is just a matter of time before he can enact control over

the target using threats such as abruptly leaving the victim and arousing the fear of abandonment. The abuser may threaten to divorce the subject or leave him/her for another partner, or the abuser may play around with these kinds of threats by talking about how desirable another person is, how he/she might like to be with that person if they weren't with the target and other situations of that kind. Doing this over and over will cause the target to doubt more and more her own capability of staying in a relationship and "keeping" a man at her side. This will build toward the degradation of self-confidence and identity, playing into a whole new level of emotional manipulation as described in the previous sections.

The tactic of pulling away, stringing along behind, then rewarding with a brief return is one way to put this tactic into hyperdrive. That period of alone time without the partner can often work to inflame that sense of fear and anxiety about the loss so that when the partner does finally throw the target a bone, she responds with desperation and a willingness to go along with anything the partner wants in order to get him back into her life.

All three of these manipulation tactics used within relationships an be effective alone or together as a combination of tactics. The decision regarding the tactic being used is often dictated by how much the target begins to show her colors regarding her own emotional vulnerabilities. The abuser who chooses to pay attention to these signals and then exploits those areas of vulnerability is a malicious type of an abuser who has chosen to put his own emotional needs and desires ahead of that of the partner or target he has chosen. Sometimes, this switch to an abusive spouse happens down the road, following a traumatic event, and sometimes, this is something the abuser will go at great lengths to hide until he is married and feels secure in his position of power and dominance over the partner. Other times, the manipulator has been an abuser his whole life, being in possession of one of the dark triad personality types. He has become an expert in this particular field and has possibly put a lot of thought and preparation into his choice of partner and how he will enact his manipulation tactics and control after the relationship has been established under false pretenses.

Just as a mother of a son who becomes a violent criminal cannot often completely lose the love and attachment for her child, the partner of an abusive partner may find it incredibly difficult to tear herself away from the situation when she has grown to truly love the abuser and has formed a strong bond and sense of attachment to him. As mentioned before, the additional factors involved, such as children, can work against the victim to keep her locked in a situation. This makes her feel trapped and as though she cannot go to anyone else for help, whether she's been threatened directly by the abuser or these fears are only in her head.

Chapter 8: Acceptable Influence vs. Toxic Manipulation

We've covered quite a bit of ground regarding the manifestations of dark psychology in society and how some of these tactics are considered to be among the malicious and psychologically damaging forms of abuse in existence. However, it is important to remember, as specified in our first chapters, that the use of dark psychology is spread over a wide spectrum of behaviors and intentions, not all of which are insidious and with the intention of inflicting harm or exploiting other people's vulnerabilities to an unethical level. The point at which this line can be drawn might differ from person to person, but, in this chapter, we will discuss how to discern between an abusive manipulator and someone who is employing a low level of manipulation with much less malicious intentions.

There is no perfect formula for deciphering what a person's intentions are or whether he is knowingly employing tactics of dark psychology. It is up to you to make decisions regarding how you will proceed with interaction when something feels amiss, and it is important that you follow your gut instincts when it comes to feelings like this. Often, the subconscious mind knows things that it cannot communicate directly to the conscious mind. So, if you feel red flags going up and your nerves are standing on end, even if you're not sure why, it is probably a good idea to remove yourself from the interaction or take steps to make sure things do not progress.

Tolerable Manipulation and Influence

Low-level manipulation tactics are those strategies which are involved in things like sales pitches and political speeches. These forms of persuasion are employed using certain information about the human psyche but are not intended to directly hurt the person or explicitly misguide them. Even in the realm of politics, where the lines between ethical use and unethical use of persuasion tactics can be blurry, the facts can be sorted from the nonfacts, and people are left to their own devices when it comes to the ultimate decision of whether to vote for a particular individual or not. However, the use of such tactics like disseminating hateful ads or intentionally divisive ads throughout social media is one tactic that has come under fire in recent days. Though you are not directly forcing a person to make a personal decision with these tactics, you are substantially altering the psychological environment that will ultimately make the decision under the stress of having been influenced in a visually staggering way. Again, the line here can be blurry, as typical political ads often try to trigger those emotional responses that we talked about during our discussion o the three modes of persuasion. Additionally, everyone is probably going to have a different opinion about where that line actually is. Should we not allow social media to throw targeted ads at us based on our data? Should we report someone in a store who is trying to get us to feel bad about not donating to such and such cause?

The best we can all do as individuals is to safeguard ourselves by being in control of the type of situations we put ourselves into and being always aware of the possibilities. Just like in our example with a salesman in a store, when a customer voluntarily walks in there, she knows that, at some point, she is probably going to be approached by someone trying to sell her something. She walks into the store even though she knows this and makes the decision that she is willing to tolerate this interaction for the sake of picking up whatever she needs. When you listen to a news show or a pair of talking heads in a debate, you know that each of them is going to try to throw arguments and facts at you in an effort to convince you of their way of seeing things, but it is up to you to actually research and make sure that what these people are saying is accurate and to make judgments and decisions for yourself. Protecting yourself means being aware of the possibilities while not outright turning yourself into a totally cynical person who never trusts anyone in any capacity. There may be an honest, young gentleman who crosses your path today needing help with a flat tire. The decision is yours as to what you will do, following this event. Do you let down your guard a little to help the man? Or do you refuse based on the fear of the unknown? Well, the answers are different for each of us. It is for us to take into account the circumstances surrounding the situation.

Play the role of the detective in order to help you discern whether a situation is reasonably safe or if there is some risk involved. Look for the signs that someone is not completely honest with you during an interaction. We've discussed some of the things you may want to watch out for during an interaction with a stranger, which may give you some clues as to whether the person is genuine or not. In addition to this, remember to take a step back and be aware of your environment at all times. Are you in a place where it might be easy for someone to catch you off guard? Next time you have to go somewhere for whatever reason at night, consider taking along a friend to ensure safety in numbers. Never offer your trust willingly when you are in a situation that feels unsafe or not completely comfortable. Listen to your gut in situations like these where it could be up in the air as to what a stranger's intentions are for talking to you.

This mindfulness about your surroundings and the circumstances of interaction should extend to online interactions as well. Never give out personal information to someone you've never met in person. Do not trust that everyone you talk to online is exactly who they say they are. A lot of people make use of dating sites and have successfully found partners online, which is a wonderful thing. However, it might be wise to stick to those most reputable sites if you decide you want to try this route for whatever reason. Signing and participating in a site that charges a monthly fee or another kind of financial commitment helps them weed out and avoid those people who are just trying to get in somewhere to meet someone and manipulate them off the cuff. Those who take their time with a profile and are willing to pay a fee for the services offered on the dating site are more likely to be genuinely invested in the endeavor.

Also, never agree to meet someone in person for the first time at a private residence or otherwise non-public place. Always assume the worst when it comes to such interactions until you have had a chance to see otherwise. Make sure that you are meeting at public places, and consider taking along a friend if you are feeling especially nervous about meeting someone for the first time. As an additional test, make sure to pay attention to the information exchanged online, though it shouldn't be personal information at this stage. Remember the likes and dislikes and the more mundane things included in the profile so that you can quiz the individual in subtle ways when you meet in person. If the person you are meeting seems to be familiar with the subject matter and recognizes immediately when you mention something from their profile, this is a good sign that they are being real with you. If you mention these things, but the person seems to struggle to maintain composure and make things up to fill in the gaps, then this could be a red flag that the information shared on his profile is not genuine and simply rehashed from another profile or made up entirely. You can never be too careful in this arena, so do what you can to stay aware. Make sure you can trust the person through in-person interaction.

Not All Intentions Are Malicious

With all of these said, it is also important to remember that people sometimes utilize subtle and minor forms of manipulation, which are not malicious in nature, as a way to present the best of themselves to someone new. It is something that is pretty universal across the young dating world. People going on their first dates are always pretty mindful of themselves and the person they are presenting, either because they are afraid to show their true selves just yet or they want to make sure they don't do something silly out of nervousness. Different personalities deal with this kind of anxiety in different ways, so don't completely  discount a person for fumbling over a few words or talking about something that is not openly discussed on their profile in the case of an online to in-person interaction. It is best not to live in complete fear of every single person you meet in person and online as if they are a potential threat to your physical and mental well-being. While this book is all about manipulation and protecting yourself from it, it is also very important to realize that living life itself is always going to involve risk, and sometimes, it is necessary to accept risks for the sake of what you might gain or the fact that you gain fulfillment and satisfaction on a very personal level from whatever activity or endeavor you are thinking of embarking on. There is no way to safeguard yourself against danger in every aspect of your life completely. If you tried to do this, you would probably end up locking yourself in a room and never venturing to experience anything else in your life. This is no way to live, so try to maintain a mental balance between being careful in your day-to-day interactions and activities while also being brave enough to live your life.

Chapter 9: Manipulative Family Members

Perhaps right alongside manipulation between romantic partners is manipulation that is exercised between family members, and this is one of the most hurtful and toxic experiences a person can go through. In this chapter, we will go over some example situations in which dark psychology can operate between family members in a home or close family members living apart. The first dynamic we will discuss is that between a parent and child.

The Child as the Manipulator

When you were young, do you remember your parents using certain tactics on you as a way to show you that something you did was wrong or to punish you? Some of us talk about the guilt factor involved when a parent would simply look really hurt and explain that she is disappointed as a way to make the child feel bad for his actions. This took the place of physical punishment, and I think a lot of us would say that this form of emotional punishment utilizing guilt and shame can be worse than a spanking.

As a child grows older, she may employ manipulation tactics in order to deceive or mislead parents so that they can do things that are normally not allowed. This is considered pretty typical behavior for teenagers to most people, though it can be infuriating and frustrating for parents trying to guide and protect their kids.

When manipulative tactics turn toxic and cause long-term harm, a vicious cycle of hurt and mistrust can form where there was once love and trust. Abusing another's love for you for the sake of getting something from them is a hurtful and damaging path. Let's look at an example to see how this might unfold.

A couple of attentive and nurturing parents raise a son named Derek. Derek is a well-behaved kid all throughout grade school and middle school, but in high school, he starts getting involved with kids who are always drinking and partying. They also introduced him to drugs. At first, he just partakes every once in a while when he is at a party, but after his first two years in high school, he realizes he has developed a kind of dependency on it and craves for the drugs several times a week. He has someone to buy from in connection with his friends at school, but he doesn't always have the money. To get cash, he asks his parents and makes up an excuse for needing money. He has not been getting in trouble with the school, and his parents do not know about his behavior outside of school. They miss him

more and more because he seems to be gone so much, but he does not really open up to them often.

In this situation, a kind of trade-off turns into a vicious cycle, and Derek picks up on how he can manipulate his parents to get what he wants because he knows what they need from him. When he needs cash, he also takes a night to spend time with them and talk to them about school and basically just tell them what they want to hear—that he is doing well and he is happy and healthy. At the end of the conversation, once he feels he has made some key connections with them, he says that he needs money for something reasonable. Maybe he says he just met a girl and wants to take her out, or he needs money to help with a project or event at school because he is part of a committee or something like that. His parents, now warmed up because they have gotten to spend a little time with him,  agree to give him some cash and are even a bit generous. After this happens, he disappears for the next two nights, perhaps texting his parents to let them know he will not be able to make it to dinner but sometimes forgetting. The cycle continues all the way through high school, and after high school, he genuinely tries to get a job but finds that his drug use puts him in a state where he can't really function as he needs to in order to keep a job, and the addiction has just grown stronger.

His parents, in this situation, are the most tragic component here in a lot of ways emotionally. They have raised a son whom they love more than anything, yet he is pulling away. They begin to suspect that he is not as healthy and happy as he was when he tried to convince them in high school. Perhaps they finally pick up on the possibility that he is doing drugs and not doing well academically around his third or fourth years of high school, so they try to talk to him, but he denies everything. He keeps asking for money and occasionally coming home and spending time with them at dinner and having conversations afterward, but he doesn't open up much about his social life, and he always asks for money at the end of it. When they are hesitant, and they ask him about where the money is going, he gets defensive, accusing them of not loving him anymore. Or he breaks down crying and trying to evoke feelings of pity and guilt so that they might relent. The parents may realize, at some point, that they are being played, but they are so torn because of their love and concern for Derek.

Unfortunately, this is not such an uncommon situation nowadays. Kids getting out of school and finding it difficult to get a good job or being inundated with influences who are into drugs and criminal activity to make money instead of working. Loving parents find themselves in a place where they wonder what went wrong, and they despair about the state of their kids, yet they are tethered unconditionally by their love and can never say no when their child comes home and asks for support because they are so desperate to spend time with him and try to break through that shell he has put up around himself. They are desperate, just as much as Derek is to get what he needs to feed his habit.

Cycles like this one can last for years and years as the parents continually try to reach the son, while the son continually comes home, begging for cash or a place to stay for a night or two. One constant thing in this cycle, which keeps feeding it, is the promise that things are going to change or that he is going to get help and be better and that he just needs some cash to help him get started. The lies and emotional manipulation continues while the parents are strung along behind, desperately hoping for a miracle and unable to shut their son out or refuse him help.

Situations like this one do not often have easy endings, though sometimes, the child successfully completes rehab and then struggles with everything he has to  change and kick his habit for good. People do this through all kinds of different support networks, sometimes religious affiliations or charity organizations where they completely reorient their focus and surround themselves with support to help them stay away from the temptations of their old lives. The cycle can be broken, but it is a hard road where emotions are involved in manipulation techniques over time.

The Parent as the Manipulator

Now, we will look at an example of emotional manipulation where the tables are turned—the child is the victim of abuse by the parent.

A young girl named Anna has grown up with her mother and a stepfather who has never really concerned himself with developing a relationship with her. The two met when Anna was 11, and now, she is 13 and getting ready for high school. Anna's mom spends as much time with her as possible, though Anna's stepfather often forms a divide between them as he introduces ultimatums about who Anna's mom will spend time with and how he will leave if she can't pay enough attention to him. In this situation, both the mother and daughter are under the influence of emotional abuse, but in different ways. The mother feels that she has a responsibility to both, though the husband tries to manipulate her into feeling as if she is neglecting their relationship. The daughter is made to feel as if she is taking time away from her mother and stepfather, and she sees the clearly visible frustration and the rage that develops whenever she comes to her mother. This happens especially when she seeks attention and support as she enters high school and is nervous about changes.

The way the stepfather maintains this kind of emotional abuse cycle is when the victim relents and gives him what he wants—mostly an admission that he is right and they are wrong and an apology. He then responds with apparent warmth and understanding and gives them just enough hope that he might be changing to keep the relationship going. The daughter is not at the point where she is going to lash out and try to yell some sense into her mother, and the mother does not yet feel that her husband's requests are inconsiderate or selfish. This is all because of the way he responds when they finally relent to his wishes. He says things like, "I'm sorry for the way I acted" or "I know I am being selfish; I just really care about you," etc. He learns over time what is effective and what is ineffective and pays attention to the reactions he gets when he uses different strategies to evoke emotional dependence and sympathy. It is an insidious thing to do in a relationship, especially when the victims are susceptible to compassion and empathy and are naïve. Both victims want to believe that they are not in a dangerous or toxic situation, and they grasp onto the kernel of hope each time a bad interaction ends. This acts like fuel that moves the situation forward as it escalates, all the while making the victims believe they are making headway and coming to an understanding.

This situation is a prime hunting ground for the manipulator who may start to use different manipulative tactics to enforce control and dominance. The stepfather may be driven by a number of different motivators that are mostly unfathomable to people who are not in that position. He may be jealous of the two young women's bond and acts out of frustration with this, trying to drive them apart and force himself between them. There may outside factors involved, as we've discussed, which lead him to act out on the only people he feels he has control over.

The danger comes into play when the cycle is broken in some way, and there is a possibility that the stepfather reacts violently as his paradigm of control over the household is shattered. Perhaps somewhere along the road, the victim realizes that things are never going to change and that the love and trust and respect that the mother once thought was there no longer exists. They decide to leave permanently and even reach out to government agencies and other family members for support. They try to plan a quiet escape, but the stepfather finds out and immediately gets angry to the point of rage.

Many tragic endings have followed such a scenario in real life, and it highlights the need for support in the area of domestic abuse victims who are trying to get out of a dangerous and toxic environment at home.

Another set of circumstances where the parent might exercise emotional manipulation is in the case of an absent parent who later comes back to ask for support from an adult child. Even when a parent is absent, there is a bond and desire for connection with the child in most cases, which might drive them to find the parent later in life to try to rekindle the relationship. In another scenario, the child is strong enough to accept that even though this person is family, they have not earned the love and respect that would have been afforded had they actually functioned like a parent in the home. When an estranged parent comes to a point in their lives when they really don't see any other means of support other than their children, things can get awkward and heartbreaking really fast.

After that initial approach, the parent usually hides the fact that they need help and pretends that the meeting is all about wanting to apologize and reintroduce himself into the child's life. He must then watch the child's response and play according to how open and willing he is to give in and let his father talk. If there is any degree of desire for reconnection or existing love even after having been abandoned, then the father might be able to latch onto this and go along with the idea that they are forming a relationship that both had missed out on while the child was growing up. This is another form of toxic emotional manipulation,

which plays on a child's love for his parents, even when they are not the best parents in the world. Just like the example above where the parents give in to a son who is increasingly absent and becoming distant in their lives, there is a very strong unconditional love that is present in many families, which can be very difficult to overcome in toxic and manipulative situations. The abuser will milk this tendency for all it's worth where their needs or desires are desperate, while the victims desperately cling to the possibility that they can change things for the better each time they are manipulated into helping out the abuser in some way.

Chapter 10: Defenses Against Brainwashing

Brainwashing is a manipulation technique in which the abuser completely alters a victim's frame of mind concerning some aspects involved with the abuser's desire or intent for the victim. To illustrate, we will look more deeply at the example of the cult which manages to grow in number through the use of recruiters and which maintains support through the use of brainwashing, which manifests in different ways and strategies.

How Is Brainwashing Accomplished?

There is an antiquated idea of what brainwashing is that is common among people who have, thankfully, never been subject to such a practice. Most people refer immediately to science fiction movies or something like that to references what they think they know about brainwashing. Contrary to some popular beliefs, brainwashing does not involve taking over another person's brain and turning them into some kind of robot. The victim does not completely involuntarily take action according to the abuser's wishes; their minds are rather conditioned over time to think a certain way based on false paradigms that are constructed and made believable by the abuser.

Others might confuse brainwashing and hypnotism, which is a completely different practice involving different intended outcomes. The hypnotist is usually a person who practices the therapy on someone who is struggling with some kind of mental ailment, such as PTSD, and is repressing memory in order to avoid addressing the issues deep inside. The hypnotist's job is to help the victim root out these repressed memories so that they can be processed in a healthy way so the victim can continue to develop emotionally instead of remaining stunted and stuck in a place without ever moving forward with their lives. Brainwashing techniques are utilized for the sake of the abuser's intents and not necessarily the victim's desire. It is a directly manipulative tactic which does not really have the victim's well-being at heart, though it can be made to look like an altruistic effort. Let's look at how something like this might play out in the cult example.

Marsha is a middle-aged woman who has worked in a factory for almost all of her working life. She has grown quite skilled in what she does, and she is minimally satisfied with the state of affairs at home, where she works alongside a husband raising their daughter, who is 8 years old. She feels empty somehow and isn't quite sure what is wrong with her, but she attempts to look for answers through an online site called MeetUp where she might find some like-minded women who are in similar circumstances as her. She has never been a religious person, but she is also open-minded about the philosophies of the world and has always had a curious mind that loves to learn about new ideas. She finds a group of women online who are advertised as a kind of social group where they get together regularly to talk and discuss things about their lives in a safe environment where no one is judged for what they share. Marsha thinks about the idea for a while before sending an email to the leader of the group for more information about the group. The first step toward an impending brainwashing attempt follows in the form of a return email from the leader. Let us call her Sam.

Sam's message is relayed in a way that oozes with warmth and understanding for why Marsha has reached out. She makes the interaction sound effortless and puts herself on the same level as Marsha, sharing that she also has a young child and was looking for some kind of social support in the form of other similar women who might understand her situation. She also says she understands the feeling of wanting something more in her life but being unsure of what exactly that something might be. She has known, met, and talked with many women who were in this boat and then strongly encourages Marsha to consider coming to one of their gatherings. The meetings themselves are explained to be low-pressure and purely social and fun in nature. There is no obligation to share any more details about one's life than she feels comfortable with. It's not really a support group or a therapy group; it's just that a lot of women have developed close relationships within the group to the point where they feel comfortable sharing things about their lives in order to get helpful feedback. Sam relays to Marsha all about how she first started the group and how she has met such wonderful women in the process. She keeps the tone in the email both light and passionate so as not to scare Marsha away with a level of intimacy but to also draw her in with the prospect of hanging out with some fun women who are refusing to let the weight of life keep them down. Sam ends the email with a friendly remark and says that she hopes to hear from Marsha soon. She includes the details for their next meeting.

After reading this email, Marsha immediately feels a sense of excitement about the prospect and immediately has a conversation with her husband to see how he might feel about it. Marsha describes the group as a bunch of women who get together and socialize and talk about their lives. It is women-only, and he turn his brow up a bit at that remark but soon decides that it seems like a harmless undertaking and encourages his wife to try a meeting or two if that is what she wants to do. He is happy that she is excited about trying this out, as he has also picked up on the fact that she hasn't been completely happy or seemed fulfilled personally for a while. So, Marsha plans to go to the next meeting.

The meeting is held at one of the members' homes, and the place feels quite cozy and inviting as Marsha enters. There are a few fragrant candles around, and as she moves into the room, every one of the women there comes forward and introduces herself with a smile. Marsha immediately feels at home and welcomed. She is offered refreshments and then invited to sit down and speak with a couple of women in the living room. There are a few different conversations evolving at once instead of one big discussion, which helps Marsha feel at ease as she was worried about being asked to speak in front of a large group. Instead, she begins conversing with a small group of three other women who listen intently as Marsha introduces herself and what's going on in her life. She already feels much more at ease as she is being listened to. The conversation continues, and the other women also talk about their lives and open themselves up in terms of vulnerability as they describe some things that they are struggling with personally. Marsha is struck by how they feel comfortable, talking about such personal things with these women, but it also makes her feel like these women could become close friends with whom she could feel confide some of her personal issues herself. She offers her own insights and suggestions as each of the ladies speak, and she begins to divulge details about her own life and her own

sense of missing something important and meaningful.

In this first meeting, there will not be any overt mention of the gathering's hidden intentions in the situation where there are any. The goal for an initial meeting is to make the potential initiate feel as safe and secure as possible. They want to surround her with warmth and make her feel like she can trust these women who only have her best interests at heart. This essential step works to encourage the victim to let her guard down and to feel like she can reveal areas of vulnerability, which will be the cult's secret weapon.

Once the women know Marsha's areas of vulnerability, they can home in on that factor as a way to gradually convince her that they can help and bring her fulfillment and happiness in all the ways she is looking for. After this initial meeting, she is likely to come back and then continue to come as something she looks forward to each week. As the meetings continue, she will start to think of these women as friends, as they also work toward convincing Marsha that they have answers to her problems. At some point when the timing is right, the women might introduce one of the cult's covert practices which involves goings-on that are quite foreign to her. But because of her developed relationship and sense of trust between the women, as well as her natural curiosity, Marsh agrees to attend and watch a ritual where the women turn their attention to some kind of deity at work, taking care of their souls and granting desires in exchange for services. Now, obviously this example is a little out there, but the focus here is on the gradual manipulation process which works to enfold a victim into a circle of warmth where things they would never have considered involving themselves in before become more and more possible because of the prior conditioning received from the women. After all, at this point, she is receiving information and suggestions from people she considers friends, and with that comes a level of trust and suspension of disbelief for their sake.

The ritual is explained in terms that are not too intimidating, and the terms are often less dramatic than how other people would define these proceedings. The word cult is never used, for example, and the words used to describe everything are soft, if not entirely inaccurate. This is slowly to let Marsha get used to the idea of what is happening without flipping a switch that starts to signal red flags. The emphasis is put on the fact that these proceedings have helped the women in the group solve their problems and find solace and peace and fulfillment—things that Marsha has also been looking for in her life. The very fact that these promises seem to be targeted directly toward her make her feel as if she has fallen into the hands of destiny, and it has finally let her find what she has been looking for. When people's deepest desires and wants are revealed and something manifests a promise of fulfillment in return, people are likely to engage in practices and belief systems that would have seemed outlandish and ridiculous in the past. But a cult never underestimates human desire for spiritual fulfillment and peace, so they have learned how to tap into the darkest corners of another person's mind in order to root out those hidden desires and needs. At his point, Marsha is all but initiated and fully involved in the cult's way of life and belief systems.

How to Avoid Brainwashing?

Knowing we are all human beings and susceptible to manipulation that targets emotions, desires, and other areas where people are generally quite vulnerable, how can you defend yourself against someone who is trying to use these against you in a brainwashing attempt? The advice here follows the advice given in the previous chapters, where potential manipulation is involved. You must maintain awareness in all situations, and consider the possibility that the people you are talking to are not who they say they are. The golden rule in situations like this is the following: If it seems too good to be true, then it probably is.

Similar to a financial scheme in which someone tricks others into investing in false promises or nonexistent entities, the person or 'business' is convinced as something where they can make a whole lot of money for very little time, effort, and personal risk. This happens a lot of the time. It is quite impossible, and people should be aware of the schemes at work in the real world, which prey on people's simple desires for money, and to get it the easy way. On a deeper level, there are those who know that they can manipulate their way into someone's heart and circle of trust by promising quick fixes for the things which plague many human beings. These are things that have to do with deep spiritual

fulfillment or finding peace or meaning in daily life, which sometimes seems like a road full of emptiness, especially when there are hardships to work through. Be aware of those deepest vulnerabilities that you harbor in yourself, and work to find your own way to fulfillment and satisfaction or meaning. Do not put yourself in other human beings where this deepest desire is concerned, because this is the gateway for emotional manipulation and brainwashing according to another person or group's will. Remember that the most important things in life are worked for and sought after for a long period of time and only with the help of those you love, trust, and respect based on your own choosing and experience with them. Do not let people, who promise answers to all your problems, come into your life because quick fixes just don't exist. Be aware of the ulterior motives that might exist. Do not reveal personal information that might be used against you, but instead, make others prove themselves trustworthy through tests of time and trial.

Now that you know the general workings behind brainwashing techniques, keep in mind that genuine relationships happen naturally and not according to a timeline. In the example above, Marsha fell into a trap based on her own feelings and was able to fall right in line according to a very short timeline where she should have been developing a meaningful relationship with these women with whom she chose to share personal information and issues. A large factor in this downfall was an element of group pressure where everyone around her was  acting a certain way, and this made her feel like she should be acting in the same way, too. And this involved divulging her deepest struggles. If something similar feels like having an impression on you and your behavior, it is best to remove yourself from the situation so that you have time to think clearly about what's going on. Anytime you feel doubt about a new interaction and acquaintance, let the people already in your life, whom you love and trust, help you work through what you truly feel regarding that budding relationship. Someone else might be able to pinpoint red flags when you are too distracted to notice them yourself.

Chapter 11: Neuro-Linguistic Programming

What Is NLP?

Neuro-linguistic programming is an area of research as well as a practice which involves the way we think as human beings in conjunction with language. Even if you're not familiar with the term, most readers will be familiar with some common mindfulness strategies which employ the elements of the NLP techniques, such as the law of attraction, cognitive behavioral therapy, and the way we talk ourselves through times of anxiety or nervousness. Think of the professor who is getting ready to go out in front of a large classroom of college students for the first time and how she might feel very nervous. To calm herself down, she walks through in her mind how she has been preparing for years, that she is completely prepared, and there is nothing to worry about, etc. All of the scenarios have the potential to encourage a change in mindset to serve the individual in specific scenarios. The process follows as the person recognizes the situation and how his brain automatically responds, then engages a strategy using language and repetition to alter how the brain will process and respond to the given situation the individual is trying to overcome.

The basis of this research involves how the brain processes and responds to information on a regular basis and the paradigms the mind forms as a response to this experience over time. First, it's important to gain an understanding of what we're talking about when we talk about how the brain processes information.

Every day, we are all inundated with information coming into our brains through our senses. This information comes in many forms, and when the brain gets overloaded with information to the point where it has to start picking and choosing what and when to process, we call this information overload. Information overload occurs all the time when we are simply surrounded by too much in the way of stimuli, and the brain simply can't process everything that is coming in. In order to make sense of the world, human beings have developed a process for categorization and prioritizing according to what we consciously and subconsciously deem as more of a priority than other kinds of information. But the brain can actually work against us in some respects when it begins to process information out of habits that have developed from negative experiences. For example, phobias can be formed based on just a single experience that occurred and made a dramatic impression on the one having the experience. Let us say a child accidentally walks straight into a spider web and immediately feels spiders crawling on his skin. The boy grows up to harbor an intense fear and anxiety around spiders, and this anxiety awakens each time he is confronted with a spider. The sensitivity could be so extreme that even the mention of spiders in conversation prompts a neurologic response, and the subject begins to feel a panic attack. His mind begins tricking him into thinking there is a spider crawling on him. These processes are our body's ways of protecting us from future harm based on past experiences, but sometimes, this process hinders us from moving forward or getting past things that are not actually real threats to our well-being. The mind and body mean well, but the subject needs to somehow alter the way in which his brain is processing this particular piece of information so that the fear and anxiety that are triggered do not hold him back from living his life with confidence. Perhaps he wants to go on a backpacking trip that will involve hiking through wooded areas, but his anxiety and spider phobia keeps

getting in the way, so he is finding it difficult to say yes to the excursion, even though he really wants to do it. The individual might be able to benefit from NLP research and tactics as a way to reprogram his mind to process this particular information differently in a way that will help him instead of hold him back.

The good news in this scenario is that research in the past few decades have discovered an innate malleability and plasticity, which are inherent in the human brain. This means that we can teach our brains to react differently if we practice a kind of cognitive re-programming in the moment. Over time and with repetition, the brain will learn to react with complacency and confidence rather than fear and anxiety, and it relearns through retraining what the subject wants to happen in those moments. The subject in this scenario might first come to terms with the idea that the fear itself is irrational and simply a product of past childhood experiences. When faced with this anxiety, perhaps through showing pictures of spiders to him, the subject will then devise some sort of monologue to go along with the experience. The monologue might entail that this challenge is about preparation instead of fear and that the anxiety is a step toward understanding instead of an anticipation of danger. The information is being received the same way mechanically, but we are rewriting the story we tell ourselves through the brain's understanding and reactions. The subject might come up with a certain behavior or mental command which will redirect the anxiety and change it into something else before the feeling gets out of hand. With time and practice, the stimulus of the spider will trigger the conditioned responses that the brain has been trained to turn to in this specific situation, thus eradicating the anxiety and fear that had once accompanied the stimulus.

Let us look at another example. Many people suffer with anxiety in a generalized way, which makes the anxiety rise at sometimes unpredictable times throughout the day, and these episodes are often accompanied by panic attacks. Panic attacks can be quite debilitating, first as the experience itself is quite uncomfortable, but also because the subject learns to be anxious about the potential of an impending anxiety attack, compounding its effect and impact on a day-to-day basis.

There are different treatments available for this kind of ailment, and rewiring the brain's response to life's unpredictable situations can be helpful in this process of alleviating as much anxiety as possible on a regular basis. The rewiring happens as the subject practices a consistent application of a narrative which is different from the one which encourages fear and doubt. For example, a subject might  teach herself to acknowledge anxiety as her body's way of readying herself for an experience as it becomes hyper-aware of everything in her surroundings. As this is supported and backed up over time and with repetition, the subject might then add in additional ways of processing information as the narrative moves along. It is a kind of misdirection which enables the subject to move in a different direction than the one that has been developed as a habit based on events and past negative experiences. The subject should work to replace these negative experiences with the positive ones in which the body's anxiety responses help bring awareness to a situation, helping the subject navigate the scenario successfully. The brain is working alongside the conscious self to improve upon a behavior in response to certain information or stimuli, and that is neuro-linguistic programming.

How is NLP Used in a Manipulation Scheme?

So how can NLP be used against a subject as part of some manipulation scheme employing dark psychology? Well, if we all know individually that we can have an impact on ourselves through language and redirecting the brain, those who have some knowledge in psychology also realize the significance of this phenomenon. The impact of language and the accumulation of that language coming from several different individuals can have a huge impact on the mindset of the target. This is why phenomena like peer pressure and groupthink have been established as clear indications of the social aspect of human beings' process of forming opinions and ideas about others and their experiences. Groupthink is the phenomenon where a group of people working together might be influenced by each to a large degree in a way that shuts down the creativity and innovation that comes from individual thought processing. An individual is pulled into the group's opinions and thought processes instead of feeling the freedom to innovate and come up with individual creative ideas because of a mix of psychological factors, such as peer pressure and not wanting to stick out or be different from the crowd. As the ideas fly around in the form of words and shared thoughts, this process becomes solidified as the brain does not make room for anything other than the information being thrown at it by other people. In this way, the potential for an innovative idea that comes from a single creative mind might be squashed under the weight of the collective thought and creation process, leading to lots of missed opportunities.

A similar phenomenon occurs when a single target is focused by those aiming to utilize NLP in order to sway the target's mind to a particular direction. The intentions and motivations behind these actions might vary from simply wanting to form a negative opinion of someone else in the target to trying to cause the target to take a harmful action toward another target. Factors such as being in a position of authority or power can have an added impact in these endeavors, and they are not always conscious endeavors on the part of the manipulators. A prime example is the high school environment.

Most of us probably remember the days when what the popular kids said about  you had a bit of impact on how other peers thought about you. If you were one of those popular kids, then you might remember how your opinions and statements about other people tended to carry a lot more weight than the words of someone who was less popular. It doesn't even matter how much evidence there was to support the claims or opinions of people; it was simply a matter of disseminating information mixed with some other influential factor, in this case, popularity. When the person with some kind of influential power speaks, people are more willing and primed to listen and form opinions in line with what they are hearing. And the more this gets reinforced, the stronger the influential factor. Gossip can be a strong manipulation tool in that people tend to be drawn toward many aspects of gossip. Gossip between peers within some kind of organization structure, like high school, makes those involved feel like they are included in something bigger than themselves, while the targets are not. It is a form of pushing others down while you boost yourself up. Sometimes, especially as a teenager, this can feel like a survival mechanism that is just absolutely necessary to your existence in school. No one wants to be the odd one out or the one everyone is gossiping about. Therefore, it pays to be part of the gossip itself while it is targeting someone else. If it is hurting someone else, that means it's not hurting you. Now, these things might not be the conscious flow of thought coming from your average teenager, but there are psychological underpinnings to all high school behavior that do not have to be consciously enacted to be effective and predictable.

One of the best practices to avoid falling into these psychological traps of influence is simply not to believe everyone you hear, especially if it is gossip! Gossip can be utilized for all the wrong reasons, and, at the end of the day, it doesn't really matter if what you are hearing is wrong or right. The reality is that you are letting secondary sources of information guide your thoughts and opinions about someone you may have never even talked to before. Don't let the allure of being included in the group draw you down in this regard. In other words, it is wise not to be drawn to others' level, especially if doing so means that you are ganging up on another human being. Think about how this would make you feel yourself; if several people started thinking erroneous things about you and developed a negative opinion without any evidence that those rumors are warranted. This is not a position you would ever want to be in, so do not inflict this position on others. A person must always be aware of the vulnerabilities and fallacies present in the nature of being human and the capacity to make mistakes and make inappropriate and inaccurate judgments toward others. One of the consistent pieces of advice appearing throughout this book is to simply be aware that you are not immune to subconscious influence. No one is too smart to be manipulated, and those who think they are, make themselves prime targets for manipulation and emotional abuse. Those who think they are the most infallible often become the weakest link when it comes to psychological practices to inflict harm simply because they do not understand the fallible nature of their minds and, therefore, never acknowledge that they need to safeguard themselves against manipulators. NLP, in the form of flattery through words, can have a huge impact on someone whose ego is already quite large. Placing yourself above others in your mind can be a quick way to a long fall, and often the victim in this scenario will not realize the truth until it is too late and they are too far down the rabbit hole.

Chapter 12: Covert Mind Control

The idea of covert mind control is wrapped in lots of different packages and sold on a variety of levels for different reasons. For example, you might see lots of online ads or videos claiming to be able to teach you to hypnotize your wife or control another person's behavior to your own ends. This type of targeted advertising might show up in social media or in websites and specifically targets those who are amateurs to the world of "mind control." They sell them the concept that in a short amount of time, you learn a few specific techniques,

develop the skills, and accomplish whatever you want.

The irony here is that this type of targeted marketing is a form of covert mind control and follows the lines of many age-old marketing and selling techniques, which are still effective today. This follows because the human being's brain and how it thinks is essentially the same, though the environment and the mode of information and how it is spread has changed drastically.

The Subliminal Message Experiment

Covert mind control is facet of dark psychology, which aspires to direct a person's actions based on subconscious commands that are planted without the targets knowing about it. The idea of hypnosis and what was called "subliminal" messaging became popular in the 70s when an interesting experiment took place with the intention of luring out an evasive killer on the loose. Here's how the experiment went down.

Law enforcement teamed up with a TV news network to broadcast a subliminal message to all who happened to be watching the show. While the reporters discussed the crimes of the killer and the details surrounding their occurrences, a very brief slide would show up on the screen for just a fraction of a second, far too fast for anyone to actually make out what it was in real time. It looked like just a blip on the screen, and most people would simply dismiss it shortly afterward. But the "blip" was actually a visual image, which contained what law enforcement hoped would be a cue that the killer would see and follow due to the subconscious embedding of a command. The message itself was quite simple. It was a command to contact law enforcement, and it contained a visual cue in the form of a pair of eyeglasses similar to a pair found at the killer's latest crime scene. At the time, it was thought that the killer kept up with the news broadcasts about his crimes and that he would surely be tuning in to this particular show. They also believed that there was a chance that subliminal messaging could be effective enough to actually get the killer to pick up the phone or perhaps walk into the station and turn himself in. The notion is quite comical nowadays, and needless to say, the tactic did not work. But there was a lot going on in those days in the realm of psychology research and practices such as profiling to help law enforcement and detectives hunt down perpetrators and killers, the likes of which the country had never seen before. The 70s were a time when the term serial killer was just beginning to be included in the language of detectives working multiple crime scenes, where the same person seemed to be making his attacks following a consistent "M.O." or modus operandi, with short breaks of varying lengths in between killings. The modus operandi referred to the exact way in which the killer carried out his murders.

The subliminal messaging tactic did not work, but the research on human psychology and mind control never ceased to continue and garner support and dedicated researchers along the way.

Art of Embedded Commands

Another form of covert mind control in practice today is the art of embedded commands. There are some similarities between the theory behind embedded commands and subliminal messaging in that the idea is to communicate with the subconscious without the subconscious mind really knowing what's going on. The same principle has been applied in the theory that says you can teach yourself things in your sleep by running certain messages through earphones worn by the subject during sleep. This experiment has been run many times for a variety of different purposes. Some people believe that a person can progress through a period of grief much more quickly through the use of such sleep therapy, while others swear that their knowledge of a foreign language has been drastically improved through letting their subconscious minds listen to narratives in the foreign language while the subject is sleeping.

Embedded commands work similarly but are instead words hidden within a larger pool of words in a way that influences the listener without the listener necessarily realizing there is influence or commanding going on. This kind of "mind control" is practiced most often and most recognizably in sales and marketing, especially online marketing in today's digital world. Ads which follow this mode of embedded messaging progress a lot like a specific argument in the mode of Aristotle's logos, as has been briefly discussed. The idea is to construct a series of statements which flow logically together and which lead the listener to end up at a point where the final argument seems like the only logical, rational conclusion to the series of arguments. These arguments are designed to feel intuitive and natural, as if nothing in the world could replace the obvious truth unfolding before you in the form of the logical procession of statements leading to a given answer.

In a marketing ad, the flow usually goes something like this.

You need something, you want something, and you have to get something that you do not already have. This need can be anything from being prettier, fitter, happier, better at getting things done at work, smarter, more impressive, etc. The list can go on and on, according to any kind of product the marketer is trying to sell. The idea is to first inspire the viewer or reader or listener to realize a certain void in his/her life which needs to be filled. Most of the time, this need does not really objectively exist in the way the ad will try to convince you it does, and with urgency. Not only do you "need" whatever it is they tell you that you need, but you also need it immediately. Once the ad has you thinking about whatever it is you are lacking, they might employ another kind of tactic to throw in so that you are solidly trapped in this way of thinking that you need something. There are several ways an ad will accomplish this. Some might show other people who have bought the product who are obviously much happier than you because of it. Others will employ the use of someone famous to tell you that you're crazy if you don't buy into the idea that you need this product, etc. Others will entice the viewer or reader with images of the product itself in all its grandeur, usually a much-exaggerated depiction in terms of visual appeal. Think of the tasty hamburger images that often accompany fast food commercials. At this point, the ad has hooked you insofar as your interest. Next, they have to pitch their answer to your dilemma. In other words, "don't despair; we know you really need this thing. That's why we have this product for you m, and it will solve all of your problems!" From there, it is a matter of direct sales pitching that will utilize different combinations of tactics. Some will state that you only have a limited time to take advantage of an offer. This prompts the sense of urgency in the potential buyer that they have to act fast, thereby encouraging an impulse buy. Other ads will compare themselves to other competitors' prices and talk about how much better their products are than the competition, etc. All of this is designed with a specific process of covert mind control at work which convinces the viewer or reader that they are making a rational decision when they decide to buy, even though the very idea of buying was implanted into their brains when they decided to read or watch the ad.

Often, we don't even get a say in whether or not we want to be exposed to such ads. This is especially true online when we are engaged in routine practices like scrolling through social media feeds. Our data is compiled and sold to companies who then can design very specific ads and images that will prompt our desire to buy things in a way that the marketers already know we are susceptible to.

Online data has become a very hot-button issue in recent years, and the arguments about the morality of online marketing and "fake news" in the form of ads on social media are particularly under fire, mainly for influencing people's behavior around political elections. These ads worked to target viewers' psychological responses to things that their data has told marketers and ad designers will work on specific individuals. The ads are often visually assaulting and are designed to trigger emotional responses that will then feed into the desired behavior targeted by the ad, such as, "vote for me," "the competition is a bad person," etc. While the viewer feels as if she is thinking and making decisions of her own volition, there is a level of covert mind control that has a lot more influence on our sensibilities than most are willing to admit. And again, this is where the main weaknesses are embedded.

Convince the public that they are making rational decisions while they are being manipulated, and you have a very powerful mechanism for effective dark psychology.

The same questions arise from the realization of these kinds of covert practices at work. How can we recognize when dark psychology is being used and what can we do to protect ourselves?

Similar to other best practices outlined in this book, one of the best ways to avoid being taken advantage of in these contexts is to stay aware of the possibility that the information you are receiving is one-sided. Do your own research and find out if all the facts are being included in the stories you regularly see on your social media feeds. Also, make sure you know all facets to be known before formulating an opinion. Online marketing, especially in the political arena, have been noted to target those who seem more "on the fence" than others. These people make up lots of populations in swing states where the political vote has been known to swing back and forth by a relatively small margin at different points in time. During the 2016 election, it was these specific areas of interest in swing states which the Trump campaign ad team was able to target with social media ads attacking Hillary Clinton and inciting attitudes nearing that of hatred against her. These tactics have been cited in recent years as one of the leading factors contributing to Trump's presidential victory that year.

How to Protect Yourself From Covert Mind Control

When you read or take notice of these kinds of ads, whether they appear automatically in your social media feeds or on other news sites, it is important that you are taking everything in with a grain of salt, and make sure to not let a single person or organization's opinion sway your own mind and opinion without a well-researched set of evidence and facts. Don't let your emotions be ignited ahead of your reasoning ability, such as with an image whose sole intent is to make you angry immediately and influence how you feel about a particular issue or news story. Remember that there are always going to be differing opinions and that it is up to you to get the full story and form your own opinions based on real evidence and how you feel personally in regards to your values, ethics, morals, etc. Put simply, don't believe everything you hear or read simply because it evokes a strong emotional response. This is a mind control tactic, and you should always be on guard when you are online and going through many news stories and information being thrown at you at a higher rate.

Another way to help guide you in your endeavor to safeguard your own mind and emotions is to have open discussion with the people in your life whom you respect and trust. Get their points of view and see where they get their information, why they believe what they believe, etc. You may disagree with some things that they are saying, but it can help you get some perspective against getting your information and opinions from talking heads online. You might hear some interesting arguments put in a way that you had never heard before, and this might prompt you to see things in a different light or at least contemplate the different possibilities and points of view out there. This is very important in forming a well-educated set of beliefs and values. Don't even be afraid to expand your horizons and listen to others, especially those you disagree with. Get all the facts and respect that different people have and that this process should be safeguarded against dark psychology tactics.

Chapter 13: Recognizing Manipulators

In this chapter, we will list several tips for you to memorize and keep close by when you want to safeguard yourself against potentially manipulative people. It helps to have these tips memorized so that you teach your brain to automatically recognize them when these warning signs appear.

They Constantly Challenge You to Prove Yourself and Show Affection

When you are dealing with someone who is constantly asking you to prove how you feel about them, there is a possibility that there is a manipulation attempt at work. People trying to manipulate you will often keep you on your toes to the point where you feel guilty when you are not giving in to their demands. This can be emotionally draining because you feel guilty that the person does not realize the extent of your compassion or love you have for them but are also confused as to how you are not doing enough. This mixture of confusion, guilt, and mental exhaustion creates a perfect hunting ground for the emotional manipulator.

They Are Passive-Aggressive

The nature of the manipulator is to slide influence in under the radar. This nature contributes to their affinity for being passive-aggressive instead of direct, even when it is incredibly hurtful and founded in spite. At the heart of this behavior is a profound fear of losing control, and not being direct means that they are not facing the consequences of a direct confrontation.

They Use Gaslighting on You

As we've discussed in previous chapters, gaslighting is a toxic manipulation tactic that works to convince the victim that they cannot rely on their own recollections and sense of reason in arguments or other situations. The victim's sense of self-awareness and confidence in her own reality is completely broken down over a period time. The practice of gaslighting is a huge indicator that this person is practicing manipulation. Be confident in yourself and what you believe happened. Don't let someone else convince you that they know better than you if you were the one with direct experience. If direct communication and addressing the situation does not work initially, the manipulator is unlikely to ever admit defeat in this regard, and it is best to remove yourself from their environment or vice versa.

They Use Humor as a Weapon Against You

Manipulators might go too far when it comes to turning a hurtful situation into something that was "just a joke." This works in their benefit if and when you choose to address it and explain that your feelings were hurt because they can come back and accuse you of being sensitive and unable to "take a joke." Don't fall for this tactic. If someone has hurt your feelings, joke or otherwise, it should be acknowledged or addressed because the pain itself is very real. It doesn't matter if it was supposed to be a joke or not.

They Are Always the Victim

People who are working as the manipulator in a relationship will often turn the "victim card" in an effort to redirect your anger and alleviate any sense of being in the wrong in the first place. This might manifest as a sudden switch from anger to sadness in the form of elephant tears and an apparent breaking down in front of you. The manipulator will quickly try to list all the ways in which she is not responsible for negative consequences and try to turn the blame around to be placed on the partner.

They Use Kindness as a Weapon

People who are out to get something from you often try to incite a feeling of obligation and a sense that you "owe" them through giving you things freely and treating you with excessive kindness and generosity. This way, the next time they need something from you, they can cite that one time they did something for you in the hopes that you will feel guilty and give in to their demands.

They Belittle Your Pain

A skilled manipulator will be able to belittle your pain by making your problems and issues out to be nothing significant. This is designed to make you feel like you should be stronger or able to handle things like everyone else, prompting feelings of guilt, shame, and especially inadequacy. The manipulator can use these feelings against you in different ways, such as making you more suggestible to their advice or to doing thing "their way." They seem stronger than you because they do not have the same struggles and recognize your struggles as those which only the weak have problems with.

They Keep Their Cool to Magnify Your Own Emotions

When something stressful happens that gets you upset, one way for a manipulator to feel superior is not to react in the same way. Instead, they handle  themselves in a completely calm and cool manner. This way, they emphasize to themselves and anyone around that you are the one losing control, while they seem to be completely unbothered by the situation. They can then come at you with an accusation that you need to work on controlling your emotions.

Chapter 14: Manipulating Manipulators

Finally, this is something you can work on to completely derail someone who is trying to manipulate you—learn how to give them a taste of their own medicine. One of the most satisfying experiences in this arena would be to catch someone completely off guard while they are in the middle of a scheme that makes them feel superior to you.

Mirror the Manipulator

One way to pull this off is to practice the art of mirroring yourself in the context of a public gathering. Now that you know how a manipulator works, you can conduct an experiment when you feel that someone is trying to use flattery and mirroring to get on your good side. To do this, simply employ the personality of someone other than yourself. Perhaps you tell jokes with exaggerated enthusiasm or adopt a super serious affect. If the person who approaches you chooses to mirror these aspects, you will notice right away because of the jarring difference between the personality you've chosen and the personality being mirroring before you. At an integral moment in the conversation, switch gears to convey your own personality, and see how this person responds. If they are thrown off, the odds are, they were trying to mirror you, and now, they don't know what to do. If they are smart, they will realize what is happening and high-tail it away from you in embarrassment. It is likely this person won't be bothering you again.

Be Immune to the Manipulator's Charms

Another way to shut down a manipulator is simply to refuse to let them get under your skin. A manipulator trying to seduce you by charming you or get you angry to prompt an outburst, make you feel guilty, make you cry, or cave in are all tactics employed by the dark psychology user. You will be able to throw the frustration on their faces when they realize that their tactics are not going to work on you as you keep a straight face and a cool demeanor. Granted, this is easier said than done.

In order to enforce this kind of awareness and control over your emotions, you must first really get in touch with and address those areas of vulnerability you see in yourself. If you are someone who empathizes and cries easily when you see others in pain, it is important to be aware that this particular vulnerability can be taken advantage of in certain circumstances. If a complete stranger approaches you and starts right in on a sob story, then it would be wise to not give in with your emotions before you can verify its validity or weed out the purpose behind this person unloading this information onto you. If the context is inappropriate, then your senses should be telling you that this person might not have the most ethical intentions.

Be Aware of Your Emotions

The bottom line here is that the best way to undermine a manipulator and throw his own tactics to his face is to remain in control and fully aware of your own emotional state. Even if it means behaving in a way that seems rude or impolite, take a moment to really think about where this particular anxiety comes from. Do you genuinely feel that defending yourself and putting up an emotional guard in certain ways is inherently "rude," or did you just buy into that idea based on what other people tell you or convey to you? What is in your best interest? Let these arguments serve you through lines of reason and personal judgment before letting other people or society tell you what is and is not appropriate in social contexts. Don't ever fall for the feeling of obligation that may lead you into a situation where you feel uncomfortable. If you've been invited to a party full of strangers and something feels off, then leave. It's as simple as that. Don't fret about what your friend will think about you or what people will say. Your safety comes first.

A word of caution before getting overtly defensive or confronting a dark psychology user is imperative here as we close this book. The very nature of a manipulator is that their emotions have some degree of volatility, and you can never know exactly how someone is going to react. Especially if you are in a situation where you are alone with the manipulator, think twice before throwing their tactics to their face. It might be wiser to play the game until you have a chance to call someone for help or get support from someone, including the police, in order to remove yourself from the situation. The scenarios will vary, and you could be in a public setting, like a party or club, and you simply wish to make it clear that you are not a good target for the manipulator's schemes. Use your common sense and judgment in these situations, and remember that even though it might make you feel good about yourself by exposing the manipulator, it is never worth putting yourself or others in danger.

Conclusion

Thank you for making it to the end of *Dark Psychology Secrets: Defenses Against Covert Manipulation, Mind Control, NLP, Emotional Influence, Deception, and Brainwashing*. Let's hope it was informative and able to provide you with all of the tools you need to achieve your goals, whatever they may be.

You now have the knowledge and know-how you need to stay on guard throughout your day-to-day life against those who might seek to manipulate you. We encourage you to share what you've learned with others so that they might also benefit from what you've learned.

The modes of persuasion and different tactics used by manipulators are no longer a great mystery to you, as you can now recognize when the warning signs appear and how to remove yourself from the situation when you feel uncomfortable. You've learned that manipulation plays on many different emotions and that no two manipulators have the exact same intentions in mind. The defense inherent in learning all about manipulative techniques is finding out that the warning signs become obvious where, previously, you may not have recognized at all what might be happening. It is important to trust your instincts and not just go with the flow at all times for fear of sticking out or being the oddball. This impulse has led many unsuspecting victims into an impending tragedy, so don't let this happen to you. Stay near to those whom you truly know, love, trust, and respect, and guard these gifts when it comes to new relationships.

It is important that, although you stay on guard against potential manipulative techniques, you also do not fall into a dark place where you no longer engage with anyone outside your own home. Do not let the fear of having to confront a dark psychology user interfere with your life and your goals. There are lots of amazing people to meet and interact with, which will add so much value to your life. the key is to simply remain steadfast in what you require from another human being before you become willing to bestow on them the level of trust and love that you have for your friends and family who are in your life now.

Remember that a lot of support can be utilized through having honest and open communication with your friends and loved ones whom you trust. There is often a great deal of wisdom to be learned from talking to those who may have actually experienced what you are afraid to confront. Be aware of your own vulnerabilities, and don't be afraid to let these trusted individuals help you with whatever emotional weaknesses you see within yourself. By doing this, you are putting up a barrier between that which you know you are susceptible to and those who might try to get on your good side and exploit that particular emotional reaction. Take advice from those who are older or more experienced, and never take for granted that just because it hasn't happened to you yet, it never will. We are all potential victims. The difference between those who avoid catastrophe and those who don't is knowledge, along with mental preparation and awareness. You've made great strides toward strengthening all three of these safeguards, and we appreciate that you've chosen to begin your journey with this book. Share what you've learned, and continue working on yourself through whatever makes you feel happy, knowledgeable, and strong.

Finally, if you found this book useful in any way, a review on Amazon is always appreciated!